THE STANDARD LANGUAGE IDEOLOGY OF THE HEBREW AND ARABIC GRAMMARIANS OF THE ʿABBASID PERIOD

The Standard Language Ideology of the Hebrew and Arabic Grammarians of the ʿAbbasid Period

Benjamin Paul Kantor

UNIVERSITY OF CAMBRIDGE
Faculty of Asian and Middle Eastern Studies

OpenBook Publishers

https://www.openbookpublishers.com

Any digital material and resources associated with this volume will be available at https://doi.org/10.11647/OBP.0382#resources

Semitic Languages and Cultures 21.

ISSN (print): 2632-6906
ISSN (digital): 2632-6914
ISBN Paperback: 978-1-80511-182-5
ISBN Hardback: 978-1-80511-183-2
ISBN Digital (PDF): 978-1-80511-184-9
DOI: 10.11647/OBP.0382

Cover image: A fragment of an unidentified dual-script (Hebrew and Arabic) grammatical-exegetical discussion from the Cairo Genizah (Cambridge University Library, T-S Ar. 31.26). Courtesy of the Syndics of Cambridge University Library. Cover design: Jeevanjot Kaur Nagpal.

The main fonts used in this volume are SIL Charis SIL, SBL Hebrew, and Scheherazade New.

أهدي هذا الكتاب إلى أستاذتي العزيزة

Kristen Brustad

CONTENTS

Acknowledgments ix

Abbreviations xii

1. Introduction 1

2. Previous Studies on the Interface between the Medieval Hebrew and Arabic Grammatical Traditions 5

    1.0. Jewish Education (Goitein 1962) 5

    2.0. Arabic Sources (Becker 1998; Basal 1998; 1999; Becker 2005) 6

    3.0. Bible and *Qurʾān* (Khan 1990; 1998) 8

    4.0. Comparative Philology (Maman 2004) 10

    5.0. Terms for Language, Bible, etc. (Harkavy 1891) 11

    6.0. Language Usage, Standard Language, and Traditional Jewish and Arab Societies (Blau 1962; 1981) 12

    7.0. Literary Genres and *Topoi* (Drory 1988; 1991; 2000; Tobi 2004) 13

    8.0. Summary 16

3. (Standard) Language Ideology as a Theoretical Framework....................18

1.0. Early Research on Language Ideology...........18

2.0. Language Ideology and Grammar..................20

3.0. Language Ideology and Performance.............35

4.0. Conclusions..37

4. Defining the Standard Language and Its Corpus..40

1.0. Cultural Possession: لغة العبرانيين 42

2.0. Exemplary Ancient Speakers: العبرانيون القدماء الأولون...54

3.0. The 'Fieldwork' *Topos*: أستمع كلام السوقة..........89

5. The Purpose of the Standard Language and the Grammarians' Mission 108

1.0. Performative Language: خطبهم وأشعارهم........108

2.0. Complaint Tradition: توجعت لنسيان الأمة اللغة...118

3.0. Blaming Foreign Languages: تَنَبَّطَتْ قراءتهم ...148

6. Conclusions..177

Works Cited 187

Index...201

ACKNOWLEDGMENTS

The research presented in this book owes its nascence to my Arabic studies with Professor Kristen Brustad—أستاذة كريستن (*ustāḏa Kristen*) as her students would call her—at the University of Texas at Austin during my Ph.D. In particular, courses on الفصحى والعامية قديما وحديثا ('Varieties and Registers of Arabic') and قراءات في التراث ('Arabic Literature in the Classical Period') introduced me to the concept of using language ideology as a theoretical framework for analysing the rich traditions and diversity of medieval and modern Arabic speech communities. Her own pioneering research in this area, which she generously shared with her students in these classes, has become a foundation for my own endeavours into the field, as in this book. Throughout my time in the classroom with Kristen, she exemplified how to approach and read a text, whether medieval or modern, in a way that has transformed and enriched my own approach to reading (especially ancient and medieval) texts ever since. The richness of classroom discussions, guided but never dominated by Kristen, cultivated then—and continues to inspire in me now—a desire to always plunge deeper into the language of the text and what it might be saying about the world of thought behind the text. All of these lessons, along with Kristen's help and extensive comments on earlier iterations of this book (and research), have been invaluable in helping it reach this point. For all of these reasons, I owe Professor Brustad my deepest gratitude.

In a similar vein, I also owe a special thanks to Phillip Stokes, now Associate Professor of Arabic at the University of Tennessee, who was a fellow student with me in Professor Brustad's classes at the University of Texas during our respective PhDs. Frequent interactions and conversations with Phillip during this time were a constant source of intellectual stimulation and growth. Especially relevant here was an offhand comment Phillip made in class one day that perhaps the Hebrew grammarians did not merely inherit grammatical conventions and concepts from the Arabic grammarians but a language ideology as well. That comment helped inspire the initial stages of this research many years ago. More recently, Phillip's insightful comments and stimulating discussions about earlier iterations of this book and the topics therein have proven invaluable in helping it reach its final form.

I would also like to thank Regius Professor Geoffrey Khan, my supervisor for my postdoctoral research at the University of Cambridge, where I have built on my earlier research from the University of Texas and expanded it into the present volume. It was actually at a presentation of mine on these topics at the American Oriental Society annual meeting in Boston back in 2016 when I first met Geoffrey—more than a year before I would join the University of Cambridge. Since that meeting, and especially during my time in Cambridge, his expertise in a variety of fields, particularly the medieval Hebrew grammarians and Judeo-Arabic, has proved an indispensable help in this area of my work. A special highlight of my time with Geoffrey has also been getting to read through portions of his critical edition of *Hidāyat al-qārī*ʾ

before its publication in a reading group he led as well as eventually helping him format the critical text edition itself. In addition to all of this, Geoffrey's insightful comments and helpful conversations on earlier iterations of my book have made the final product of better quality.

Finally, I am also indebted to my colleagues, some former and some current, from the Department of Middle Eastern Studies at the University of Texas at Austin and the Hebrew and Semitics division of the Faculty of Asian and Middle Eastern Studies at the University of Cambridge. Ongoing conversations about Biblical Hebrew, the medieval Hebrew reading traditions, the Hebrew and Arabic grammarians, medieval Arabic literature, and more have undoubtedly fed into making this a higher quality work.

ABBREVIATIONS

ACC	accusative
BCE	Before the Common Era
c.	century
ca	circa
CA	Classical Arabic
CE	Common Era
d.	(year of) death
H	high language variety
L	low language variety
lit.	literally
MS	manuscript
MSS	manuscripts
MSA	Modern Standard Arabic
n.	footnote
NOM	nominative

1. INTRODUCTION

As a discipline, the study of Biblical Hebrew grammar began largely among Arabic-speaking Jews of the Middle Ages. While the discipline has grown and evolved since then, the legacy of these first grammarians has had a lasting impact on how Biblical Hebrew is understood and taught to this day. Moreover, it is well established that the Hebrew grammatical tradition, in many ways, grew up out of and alongside the Arabic grammatical tradition. Many of the concepts present in Hebrew grammar today have their origins in Arabic grammatical concepts of the Middle Ages. This is perhaps nowhere more apparent than in the conceptualisation of a triliteral root and verbal stems/patterns (*binyanim*).[1] It is no wonder, then, that so much scholarship has been devoted to documenting the medieval Hebrew grammarians' understanding and conceptualisation of Hebrew grammar.

And yet, as recent linguistic and anthropological work has shown, setting down 'the grammar' of a language can be as much an ideological or political activity as an academic one. In addition to the language itself, speech communities also share beliefs and attitudes *about* that language, and these can have a dramatic impact on what forms of the language one regards as acceptable and what sort of rules one imposes on and through their descrip-

[1] It is significant to note, however, that some of the early Hebrew grammarians did not actually conceive of the root and pattern in this way. It was Ḥayyūj who championed the triliteral root in the Hebrew tradition.

 https://doi.org/10.11647/OBP.0382.01

tion of the language. Nevertheless, despite the relevance of language beliefs and attitudes for the foundations of grammar, more attention could still be devoted to describing the beliefs and attitudes of the early Hebrew grammarians about Hebrew and Biblical Hebrew—that is, what linguistic anthropologists would call their 'language ideology'—in a systematic way.

Indeed, while much work has been done on the interface between Hebrew and Arabic grammar and literature in the Middle Ages, these (ideological) aspects of language have yet to be treated theoretically or systematically, and are usually only discussed in isolation and/or as they relate to other wider topics. This less trodden area of scholarship is all the more apparent when we consider the fact that it may not have been only grammatical concepts or literary genres that the medieval Hebrew grammarians inherited from the Arabic grammatical tradition, but a way of thinking about language as well. If this is the case, then understanding the language ideology—rather, ideologies—of the Hebrew grammarians of the Middle Ages is essential to understanding the nature of their grammatical work and the wider sociolinguistic contexts in which it was carried out. It may even cause us to reconsider how we regard and interpret their grammatical descriptions of the language, which have come to impact many subsequent generations of students and scholars of Biblical Hebrew.

In this book, then, we will consider aspects of language ideology that appear to be shared between the Hebrew and Arabic grammarians of the Middle Ages, in particular those who were active during the ʿAbbasid period. The corpus will primarily include introductions to various Hebrew grammatical treatises—or works that somehow relate to language—written by Hebrew grammarians. Because this book intends a comparison with the medieval Arabic language ideology, the corpus will be limited to those Hebrew grammarians who composed their works in Judeo-Arabic during the ʿAbbasid period (750–1258 CE), which witnessed the most significant developments for the codification of grammar in both traditions. Such a study is significant in that it sheds further light on the relationship between the language ideologies of the Hebrew and Arabic grammarians, whether that relationship is best described as one resulting from direct influence or merely as one resulting from a common language culture. It also places the ideological history of the Hebrew grammatical tradition within its wider (Arabic) cultural and sociolinguistic contexts.

After a brief overview of previous scholarship on the interface between Hebrew and Arabic grammar and literature in the Middle Ages (chapter 2), we will introduce the concept of language ideology as a theoretical framework (chapter 3). In particular, we will describe certain features of what has come to be regarded as a 'standard language ideology' (chapter 3, §2.1). This will serve as the analytical framework through which we will then treat several shared features of a standard language ideology among the Hebrew and Arabic grammarians. While more similarities could be found, we focus on six key points of ideological similarity in this book. First, we consider language as a cultural possession of its speakers (chapter 4, §1.0). Second, we look at how certain 'exemplary speakers' of a fixed ancient corpus of texts serve as the standard for determining proper language use (chapter 4, §2.0). Third, we look at the 'fieldwork' *topos* of the grammarians venturing out 'off the beaten path' to find reliable contemporary informants (chapter 4, §3.0). Fourth, we call attention to the performative contexts with which the grammarians associate language use (chapter 5, §1.0). Fifth, we outline how the genesis of grammar is portrayed as a response to the deterioration of language proficiency among the masses (chapter 5, §2.0). Finally, we examine the negative attitude of the grammarians towards foreign languages and their influence on language proficiency (chapter 5, §3.0). Taken all together, these various strands of ideological similarity cohere to form what may be termed, following Milroy (2001, 530–31), a 'standard language culture' in each grammatical tradition.

While it lies beyond the scope of the present work to treat any of these topics comprehensively, this overview will demonstrate that the Arabic grammatical tradition influenced far more than the grammatical terms and concepts that would develop in the Hebrew grammatical tradition. Rather, it had a profound impact on the early Hebrew grammarians' beliefs and attitudes about language and their language heritage itself. In turn, these beliefs and attitudes about the Hebrew language shaped how they described and established the grammar thereof.

2. PREVIOUS STUDIES ON THE INTERFACE BETWEEN THE MEDIEVAL HEBREW AND ARABIC GRAMMATICAL TRADITIONS

The interface between Hebrew (and/or Jewish) and Arabic (and/or Muslim) grammar and literature in the Middle Ages is a well-documented phenomenon (see, e.g., Becker 1998; 2005; 2013; Drory 2000). Nevertheless, most of the attention has been garnered by shared grammatical concepts and literary genres. Specific treatments of shared beliefs and attitudes about language—i.e., language ideology—are less common.[2] When they do occur, comments that may fit into the framework of language ideology are often made in passing in works devoted to broader topics. In the present chapter, then, we will outline the relevant portions of a brief selection of previous scholarship as it touches on matters related to the interface of language ideology between the medieval Hebrew and Arabic grammarians.

1.0. Jewish Education (Goitein 1962)

One of the earliest relevant pieces of scholarship related to our topic is Goitein's (1962) סדרי חינוך בימי הגאונים ובימי הרמב"ם: מקורות חדשים מן הגניזה (*Sidre ḥinux bime hageonim uvime harambam: meqorot ḥadašim min hageniza*) '*Jewish Education in Muslim Countries—*

[2] For the definition of language ideology, see chapter 3.

 https://doi.org/10.11647/OBP.0382.02

Based on Records from the Cairo Genizah', in which he marshalls the documentary evidence from the Cairo Genizah to shed light on various aspects of Jewish education in Arab cultures during the Middle Ages. Although not directly concerned with interface of language ideology, one of the important findings of Goitein's work is that Jewish students were generally required to develop eloquent proficiency in both Hebrew and Arabic. Presumably, then, in being exposed to the grammatical literature that developed in the Muslim world for teaching *al-ʿarabiyya*, learners would also have been exposed, if indirectly and covertly, to the ideologies that underlay it.

2.0. Arabic Sources (Becker 1998; 2005; Basal 1998; 1999)

On this point, we should also mention the works of Becker (1998; 2005) and Basal (1998; 1999), who identify the various Arabic grammatical sources utilised in the works of the medieval Hebrew grammarians Jonah ibn Janāḥ (ca 990–ca 1050 CE), Abū al-Faraj Hārūn (first half of 11th c. CE), and Isaac ben Barūn (d. 1128 CE).

In the case of Jonah ibn Janāḥ's *Kitāb al-lumaʿ*, for example, Becker argues that Ibn Janāḥ imitated the overall shape of contemporary Arabic grammars. What is more, he even replicated a large number of grammatical rules and definitions by merely replacing the Arabic examples with Hebrew. Becker also identifies specific Arabic grammatical works on which Ibn Janāḥ based his work, such as *al-Kitāb* by Sībawayh (d. ca 796 CE) and *Kitāb al-muqtaḍab* by al-Mubarrad (d. 898 CE).[3]

In the case of Isaac ben Barūn's *Kitāb al-muwāzana bayn al-lugha al-ʿibrāniyya wa-l-ʿarabiyya* 'Book of Comparison between the Hebrew and the Arabic Language', he finds explicit references to *Kitāb al-ʿayn* by al-Khalīl ibn Aḥmad (d. 786/791 CE), *Maʿānī al-qurʾān* (though the title is not mentioned) by al-Farrāʾ (d. 822/823 CE), *Kitāb al-nabāt* by Abū Ḥanīfa (d. 895 CE), and numerous other well-known works of the Arabic grammatical tradition. Though without an explicit reference, ben Barūn also makes use of the famous *al-Kitāb* by Sībawayh (d. ca 796 CE). In his analysis of the material, Becker notes that the grammatical terminology used in the Hebrew grammatical tradition consists mostly of calques or pure transliterations. Moreover, even the way that ben Barūn builds his linguistic arguments—quoting ancient sources in Hebrew and Arabic (i.e., Bible, *Qurʾān*, poetry) for exemplification—follows the pattern of the Arabic grammarians.[4]

In the case of Abū al-Faraj Hārūn's (first half of 11th c. CE) *al-Kitāb al-muštamil*, Basal demonstrates that there was strong reliance on Ibn al-Sarrāj's (d. 928/929 CE) *Kitāb al-uṣūl fī al-naḥw*. In addition to cases where Abū al-Faraj appears to correct the version of Ibn al-Sarrāj he was working with, there are a number of other pieces of evidence that support this. It appears that the overwhelming majority of Abū al-Faraj's syntactic theory is based on that of Ibn al-Sarrāj, some portions of which were even copied

---

[3] For an evaluation of Becker's work, see Maman (2004, 10).

[4] For a review of Becker's work, see Shivtiel (2007).

word for word. The overall structure and order of chapters also exhibits considerable similarity. Finally, in many cases, Abū al-Faraj appears to simply replace Arabic examples with Hebrew ones that parallel (in meaning) the Arabic originals of Ibn al-Sarrāj. If Ibn al-Sarrāj quotes the *Qur'ān*, Abū al-Faraj quotes the Bible.

The work of Becker and Basal makes clear just how heavily the Hebrew grammarians depended on Arabic grammatical sources. In the words of one reviewer of Becker's work—though it could perhaps apply to each of the grammarians—"the influence of the Arabic sources is so significant that one may have the impression... that Ben Barūn's book was in fact a discussion of Arabic grammar and lexicon with illustrations from biblical Hebrew" (Shivtiel 2007, 398–99). Though more focused on grammatical concepts than language ideology, establishing such a close connection between the Hebrew and Arabic grammatical traditions opens the door for a very plausible endeavour of identifying linguistic ideological similarities as well.[5]

3.0. Bible and *Qur'ān* (Khan 1990; 1998)

Indeed, Khan (1990; 1998) has demonstrated just such an ideological interface between the attitude of the Hebrew grammarians towards the text of the Bible (and its oral reading) and the Arabic grammarians towards the text of the *Qur'ān* (and its oral reading).

---

[5] For a summary of the influence of the medieval Arabic grammatical tradition on the Hebrew grammarians, see Becker (2013).

Dealing specifically with the work *Kitāb al-anwār wa-l-marāqib* by Jacob al-Qirqisānī (first half of 10th c. CE), Khan notes a number of ideological parallels between al-Qirqisānī's views of the various Biblical Hebrew reading traditions and Muslim views of *Qurʾānic* reading traditions.

In disputes about inconsistencies between the written text and the oral reading tradition of the Bible, al-Qirqisānī ascribes authority to that which has been transmitted (*naql*) by the nation as a whole and is thus validated by consensus (*ijmāʿ*). In cases where there is no general consensus across the entire nation—as with differences between the 'Palestinian' (i.e., Tiberian) and Babylonian reading traditions—it is the Tiberian tradition that is regarded as authoritative. In this respect, the community that remained in 'the Land' is regarded preferentially for determining consensus.

A similar pattern of thought is also evidenced in Muslim attitudes towards the text and reading of the *Qurʾān*. Among the first generations of *Qurʾān* readers, grammatical considerations were primary in determining the reading of the fixed ʿUthmānic consonantal text. Over time, however, additional criteria beyond grammaticality and compatibility with the consonantal text were introduced. Proper *Qurʾānic* readings had to comport with those of renowned readers of previous generations and have majority acceptance. As a result of this development, grammarians like Sībawayh (d. ca 796 CE) and al-Farrāʾ (d. 822/823 CE) were prone to accepting certain readings of the *Qurʾān* even if they seemed less grammatical. In some cases, however, the principle of majority acceptance led to some tension and thus had to be restricted. Rather than majority or consensus applying to the nation as a whole, it was limited to certain authoritative groups of readers from particular centres, such as Kūfa, Baṣra, the Ḥijāz, Medina, and Mecca.

In both the Hebrew and Arabic traditions, then, the proper text and reading was ideally determined based on the 'majority principle'. Because this principle gave rise to some tensions when scholars were faced with different conflicting readings, however, it could be replaced (or somewhat modified) by ascribing authority to certain traditions in what may be termed the 'tradition principle'. This shared pattern of thinking likely indicates that the permeation of Arabic grammatical thought was not merely in terminology or concepts but in the realm of ideology as well.

4.0. Comparative Philology (Maman 2004)

Maman's (2004) work on *Comparative Semitic Philology in the Middle Ages* is dedicated to the grammatical theory of those medieval Hebrew grammarians who engaged in comparative philology. These philological discussions, however, touch on aspects of language ideology. Primary among them are the very terms used to refer to the languages in question. The fact that both the Hebrew grammarians and the Arabic grammarians use the terms *lisān al-ʿarab* 'language of the Arabs' and *kalām al-ʿarab* 'speech of the Arabs', often in reference to ancient Arabic speakers, is significant. The parallel use of *lughat al-ʿibrāniyyīn* 'language of the Hebrews' to refer to Hebrew speakers of the biblical and mishnaic periods constitutes an important parallel that indicates an underlying similarity of how those grammarians conceived of these languages (Maman 2004, 53–55). This will be picked up again in chapter 4, §1.0.

5.0. Terms for Language, Bible, etc. (Harkavy 1891)

On this point, it is also worth noting that some editions of the works of the Hebrew grammarians may contain comparisons with the Arabic grammatical tradition, such as those regarding terms for the language, the sacred text, the title of a grammatical work, and other central figures in the history of the language. Note, for example, how in Harkavy's (1891, 32 n. 3) edition of *Sefer Ha-Galuy* and *Sefer Ha-Egron*, he calls attention to the fact that elements of the title of Saadia's grammar resemble those of Arabic grammarians: (i) using *al-lugha* 'the language' to refer to Hebrew without a modifying adjective and (ii) using *faṣīḥ* to refer to the particular register of the language codified. He also notes how various Hebrew grammarians refer to the Bible as *al-Qur'ān* 'that which is read; the recitation'. Finally, he points out that various Hebrew grammarians refer to Moses as *al-rasūl* 'the messenger', co-opting the common term for Muhammad. While all of these points are relevant for constructing the language ideology of the Hebrew grammarians, they are still largely restricted to specific concepts and terms.

6.0. Language Usage, Standard Language, and Traditional Jewish and Arab Societies (Blau 1962; 1981)

A number of important points related to language ideology appear in the works of Blau. First of all, in a review of Goitein's work (Blau 1962), he highlights how the linguistic practices of medieval Jewish communities in Muslim societies involved a complex 'mosaic' of Hebrew, 'Middle Arabic', and Classical Arabic. While 'Middle Arabic' had become the default spoken language for Jews in Muslim lands, in large part due to urbanisation of the population, Hebrew was still maintained as a language of study, especially in and for certain religious contexts. At the same time, because Arabic had generally replaced Aramaic in the realms in which it had been previously used among the Jews, (Classical) Arabic also served as a language of study and composition. Nevertheless, because the Jews did not generally learn Classical Arabic to the depth required to compose poetry—and the typical settings and themes for Classical Arabic poetry did not transfer well to the Jewish context—the Jews still favoured Hebrew for poetic composition. From an ideological perspective, this suggests that the cultural 'fit' of a particular genre could determine language use for the medieval Jewish community. We should also note here that the preference for Hebrew in the composition of poetry has relevance for a particular aspect of language ideology to which we will return later in this volume (see chapter 5, §1.0).

Also significant for our purposes is Blau's development of the concept of a 'traditional society', a term he uses to describe both medieval Jewish and Muslim communities. In his work on *The Renaissance of Modern Hebrew and Modern Standard Arabic*, Blau (1981, 9–13) defines a 'traditional society' as a society "based on religion with which the standard language was closely interwoven." For Blau, this entails a parallel between the Bible (and Talmud) in Jewish society and the *Qurʾān* in Arab society, both of which were strongly connected with the standard language. From the perspective of medieval language ideology, this is a prevalent concept that we will see echoed later on in the present work. The concentricity of 'ancient' sacred texts and the standard language is indeed present in the language ideologies of both the Hebrew and Arabic grammarians (see chapter 4, §2.0). Nevertheless, while Blau's insight into this phenomenon is undoubtedly ahead of its time, his description of it does not benefit from more recent advances in the field of linguistic anthropology regarding standard language cultures.

7.0. Literary Genres and *Topoi* (Drory 1988; 1991; 2000; Tobi 2004)

The existing scholarship that may come closest to the goals of the present work is perhaps Drory's (1988; 1991; 2000) treatment of the impact of Arabic literature on medieval Jewish literature and culture. A number of (primarily literary) points of similarity relevant for or related to language ideology are cited throughout her work.

Drory calls attention to cases where Jewish culture adopted and/or adapted existing Arabic literary genres (e.g., the *maqāma*), which points to interface of a certain type. The concept of a canonical text corpus centred around one sacred text—the Bible in Jewish culture[6] and the *Qurʾān* in Muslim culture—also appears to be a feature of the Arabic grammatical tradition adopted initially by the Karaites and popularised by Saadia Gaon. This appropriation of Arabic models in the Jewish literary system applies to concepts, organisation, and writing models (2000, 135). These points have relevance for a number of topics treated later in the present volume (see, e.g., chapter 4, §2.0).

Drory also argues that a diglossic configuration of language usage is another similarity that exists between the two medieval cultures. For her, both Jewish and Muslim communities utilise a classical language (Hebrew or Classical Arabic) for performative, festive, and formal contexts, in a diglossic environment where another language (Judeo-Arabic or Colloquial Arabic) is utilised for simple communicative functions (2000, 158–79). We will return to and elaborate on this idea later in the book.

But perhaps the clearest case of interface between the Hebrew and Arabic grammatical traditions identified by Drory, as relevant for our purposes, occurs in her treatment of *topoi* associated with grammarians accessing linguistic informants. She recalls the fact that Arabic grammatical literature is replete with examples of the well-known *topos* of grammarians seeking out Bedouin informants for linguistic examples. After all, the Bedouin were regarded as untouched by the corruption and/or modernisation attached to more urban forms of the language and thus the

---

[6] This should be contrasted, however, with the prominent or even predominant role of the Talmud in Rabbanite Judaism.

preserve of ‘pure’ and ‘unadulterated’ Arabic. The Arabic grammarians therefore had to venture out into the desert to seek out contemporary sources for *al-ʿarabiyya*. According to Drory, this *topos* was appropriated into the Hebrew grammatical tradition and applied to the Hebrew of the inhabitants of Tiberias and the Tiberian reading tradition. This is perhaps nowhere clearer than in the text published by Allony (1970) recounting ʿEli ben Yehudah ha-Nazir’s trip to Tiberias to determine the proper pronunciation of the Hebrew letter *resh*. Indeed, Drory (2000, 141) notes that the exemplary status of the Tiberians and the Tiberian reading tradition “is not just an isolated theme that was borrowed from the Arabic and adapted into the Jewish cultural system, but rather a full ideological paradigm.” For Drory (1988, 138–49; 2000, 7, 35–36, 84, 140–42), it is not just the ‘fieldwork’ *topos* but rather the whole ideology of the prestige of the Tiberian tradition that is built on an Arabic model. This discussion will be picked up again in greater detail in chapter 4, §3.0.

It should also be noted that, while Drory appears to be the scholar who has worked most extensively in this area, there are other scholars who have touched on the interface between medieval Hebrew and Arabic literature as well. Note, for example, that Tobi (2004) has a produced an entire volume addressing the link between Hebrew and Arabic poetry in the Middle Ages. Of particular note in this volume are Tobi’s (2004, 55–58) comments on the role of the Bible and *payṭanim* in Jewish culture—particularly in the thought of Saadia Gaon—and the *Qurʾān* and ancient poetry in Muslim culture for supplying exemplary language to be imitated. As part of this discussion, Tobi also calls attention to the fact that Saadia hoped to restore the use of Biblical Hebrew to the Jewish community, at least in part due to national and religious motivations. These observations have relevance for a number of sections in the present work, which we will pick up again later (e.g., chapter 4, §2.0; chapter 5, §2.0).

8.0. Summary

While there does not appear to be any one specific work in previous scholarship devoted to the interface of the Hebrew and Arabic grammatical traditions with respect to language ideology, the preceding review demonstrates the validity of such a topic. In addition to a number of adjacent or related topics, such as Jewish education in a Muslim context, we find a number of points of linguistic ideological interface identified in the literature. Some of the most prominent among them concern the ideology surrounding sacred texts with their oral reading, the formation of the canon around an 'ancient' sacred text, and the appropriation of a sort of 'fieldwork' *topos* for retrieving reliable linguistic examples.

Nevertheless, there are many more strands of linguistic ideological interface that can be explored between the Hebrew and Arabic grammatical traditions. This scholarly review has merely served to call attention to the fact that the Hebrew grammarians' connection with and reliance on the Arabic grammatical tradition is so profound as to impact (perhaps even subconsciously) language ideology. Beyond mere quantity of examples, however, it is also worth noting that much of the previous literature has not availed itself of the advances in the field of linguistic anthropology regarding language ideology as a theoretical framework. For this reason, we will briefly address this body of literature (and its relevance for our research topic) before proceeding to analyse the primary material of this study in the remainder of this book.

3. (STANDARD) LANGUAGE IDEOLOGY AS A THEORETICAL FRAMEWORK

Put simply, a language ideology may be regarded as *the collection of beliefs and attitudes one has about their own language and/or the languages of others*. Naturally, these beliefs and attitudes shape and dictate the relationships between speakers and languages (Cavanaugh 2020, 52). Although language ideologies have tremendous power to shape society, politics, and even history—especially in the case of Hebrew and Arabic—little has been done in the way of applying linguistic anthropological theory regarding language ideology to the writings of the early Hebrew grammarians. Moreover, the fact that the language ideology exhibited in the medieval Hebrew grammarians exhibits considerable similarity with that of the medieval Arabic grammarians raises questions about possible interface and/or influence between the two. Before proceeding to analyse the primary material from the Middle Ages, then, we will first present a brief overview of the relevant literature on language ideology (and related topics) of recent decades. This will serve as the theoretical framework through which we will conduct our analysis of the primary material in the remainder of the book.

1.0. Early Research on Language Ideology

Some of the earliest work on language ideology grew out of a wider interest in power dynamics in human interactions. While this interest has long been present in scholarship with respect to

 https://doi.org/10.11647/OBP.0382.03

political and economic power (e.g., Foucault, Bourdieu), it was not until the 1970s and 1980s that linguists started to apply this same type of framework to explain different aspects of language use. Initially, this new approach was utilised by scholars such as Urla to better understand the struggles of minority languages. Eventually, however, it was expanded by linguistic anthropologists (especially Gal, Heller, Hill, Irvine, Silverstein, and Woolard) to address how language functions in forming relationships, motivating action, and structuring society at large. It was in this early literature that the concept of a language ideology was first explored to encapsulate the constellation of beliefs, attitudes, usage patterns, and power dynamics at play in a given linguistic context and language community. It was finally in 1994 that Woolard and Schieffelin published a seminal piece entitled 'Language Ideology', in which they defined the concept and explained its relevance, thus establishing it as a worthy field of study in its own right. This article would be followed by two edited volumes on the subject (Schieffelin et al. 1998; Kroskrity 2000), which continue to serve as foundational works in the field to this day.[7]

Despite its origins, however, it should be noted that language ideology is unlike political ideology. While political ideologies are typically the product of the conscious choices of those who hold them, language ideologies consist of ideas and attitudes that are embedded in the shared culture of a speech community. A proper analysis of language ideology may thus unearth features

[7] This brief review is based on that of Cavanaugh (2020, 53–54).

of a particular community's beliefs and attitudes towards language of which they are unaware themselves.

2.0. Language Ideology and Grammar

One area especially relevant for our present purposes concerns the role of language ideology in establishing, defining, and/or reinforcing the grammar of a language, as well as the power dynamics at play in such processes. In this respect, there are two relevant phenomena covered in the literature, namely that of a standard language ideology and that of enregisterment, each of which will be treated in turn.

2.1. Standard Language Ideology

Codifying the grammar of a particular language is rarely a value-neutral endeavour. Throughout history, such processes of codification have involved some degree of standardisation of language. The term standardisation generally refers to the process of imposing uniformity over what would otherwise be diverse and variegated. Language standardisation, then, involves the imposition of certain grammatical rules over what would otherwise exhibit considerable linguistic variation (Milroy 2001).

The concept of a standard language ideology, which was pioneered by Milroy and Milroy (1999; see also Milroy 1999; 2001), is thus predicated on the belief that a single *ideal* form of a particular language is superior to the others. As such, it can serve as a measuring stick against which to judge other forms of the language. Part and parcel with this belief is the idea that there exists an idealised or standardised iteration of the language outside of the community of its speakers. Although such a belief is common in many modern cultures (e.g., English, French, Spanish), not all linguistic communities may be regarded as "standard language cultures" (Milroy 2001, 530–31).

At this point, it is germane to make a brief aside about standard language ideologies in those communities characterised by diglossia, a concept first articulated by Ferguson more than sixty years ago.[8] In diglossic societies, in which a more prestigious high language (H) exists alongside a more colloquial low language (L), it is necessary to differentiate between the H language and the 'standard' language. Although the H variety of the language and the standard language are often identical, this is not always so (Ibrahim 1986). Some linguistic communities are

[8] In 1959, Charles Ferguson penned his seminal and oft-cited article 'Diglossia', in which he claimed that numerous speech communities utilise two distinct varieties of their language: a high (or standard) variety (H) for speeches, lectures, media, poetry, etc., and a low (or colloquial) variety (L) for informal conversations, interactions with waiters, folk literature, etc. While this article has become a staple in the field, subsequent scholars have tended to draw too sharp a distinction between H and L. In reality, not all linguistic specimens in such societies are clear examples of either H or L. In many (or most) cases, actual language use exists on a spectrum and is conditioned by both context and competence. In some instances, speakers may even intentionally make use of a limited set of specific features ideologically associated with H or L to achieve certain goals or meet certain expectations. Moreover, as Brustad (2017) has shown in the case of Arabic, sometimes the identification of supposed 'diglossia' itself is actually an ideological construct and not consistent with actual language use.

home to diverse dialects and registers without an overarching belief that a certain set of rules or standards should be imposed on them to create conformity with an idealised version (Milroy 2001, 530–32). We should also mention, however, that language ideology often plays a role in the identification of 'diglossia' in a given society. While in some cases diglossia is obvious and coheres with reality—take, for example, Latin as the H language vs a given local vernacular as the L language in pre-modern Europe—there are other instances in which identifying 'diglossia' in a society may itself be an ideological construct. In fact, Brustad (2017) has argued persuasively that the diglossia binary between *fuṣḥā* and *ʿāmmiyya* in descriptions of Arabic is the product of language ideology rather than an accurate description of real language use.

With the (sometimes applicable) distinction between the H language and the 'standard' language in mind, we may note some of the characteristics associated with a society possessed of a standard language ideology outlined in the literature (Woolard 1998; Milroy 2001; Agha 2003).

2.1.1. Cultural Possession

In standard language cultures, language is not so much regarded as merely a tool for communication but as a heritage to be possessed. Like laws, customs, or even religion, **the language is regarded as a 'cultural possession'** rather than a product of human interaction and cognitive abilities. At the same time, however, this cultural possession is not innate in the speakers who grow up in the society. Rather, the correct form of the language—

even one they already speak—must be taught to them (Milroy 2001, 537–38). It is also worth noting that, when language is treated as a cultural possession, it necessarily takes on certain moral aspects (see, e.g., Milroy and Milroy 1999, 8–9, 41). Preserving the cultural possession is a moral imperative for the society. Those who are proficient or eloquent in the standard language—i.e., those most invested in preserving it properly—are thus endowed with a certain moral authority. Note that elements of morality can also be reflected in how the complaint tradition manifests itself (see §2.1.5).

2.1.2. Single Uniform Language and Group Identity

Moreover, as the cultural possession of a particular (ethnic, religious, political, etc.) group, **the idea of a single uniform language is often advocated for and/or utilised to strengthen a sense of group identity and unity** (Milroy 2001, 549–50). Just as a standard language may be viewed as a cultural possession, so also the cultural identity of a particular group may require a standard language to reinforce it. Whether or not the canonical form is or ever was used among the majority of speakers in a particular linguistic community, there is a belief that it is indeed 'the language' of the ethnic group. It is often this tie between group identity and language that leads to a negative attitude towards foreign languages and their influence on the canonical standard. Frequently, such an attitude is instantiated in language authorities advocating for a rarely used 'native' vocabulary item over a commonly used loanword.

2.1.3. Abstract External Entity

Indeed, on this point, it is worth noting that standard language cultures are characterised by a belief that **the language exists in an ideal, canonical form outside of the production of the speakers who use it**. The rules, grammar, and norms of the language are properly seen as being external to the speaker. As a result of this belief, certain forms of the language can be deemed 'correct' or 'incorrect' irrespective of their practical functionality among or mutual intelligibility to other speakers in the society (Milroy 2001, 537–38). The forms and structures most commonly used among a majority of speakers can thus still be deemed 'incorrect' or 'improper' language use.

2.1.4. Neglected among the Masses

Implicit in the trends noted above is the idea that most native speakers are not faithful keepers of the language. Rather, **there is a belief that the pure form of the language is either neglected or even corrupted among the masses**. In such cases, there is a widespread opinion that without universal support and protection, the language will undergo—and is perhaps already undergoing—decline and decay (Milroy 2001, 537).

2.1.5. Complaint Tradition

This leads to what Milroy and Milroy (1999; see also Milroy 1999, 20; 2001, 538) have termed **'the complaint tradition', which involves language users bemoaning the state of the (standard) language among the wider population**. While such complaints often emanate from 'authoritative' voices on language, one does not have to be proficient in the standard to decry its decay among the wider population. There can be a sort of self-deprecatory 'complaint tradition' among more typical language users. On this point, it should be noted that such beliefs are not altogether unfounded. As a cultural possession, some forms of the language may require special care to be preserved for generations to come. The complaint tradition thus serves an important role with respect to the maintenance of the standard language (Milroy 2001, 538).

2.1.6. Legitimisation and Maintenance

The concept of standard language maintenance is closely related to the process of legitimisation. **Both social and political forces confer legitimacy on a particular 'standard' form of the language and then maintain it**. In addition to the complaint tradition, which serves to direct public opinion towards maintaining the standard language, more practical steps can be taken as well. In some cases, this involves imposing or structuring a school curriculum that privileges teaching of the standard language. The codification of a long tradition through "authoritative accounts of the language" like grammar books and dictionaries also serves to maintain and legitimise the canonical form of the language (Milroy 2001, 538–39).

2.1.7. Institutionalisation

We might also refer to some of the more structured aspects of this process as 'institutionalisation'. Though largely overlapping with legitimisation and maintenance (see §2.1.6), **we may regard institutionalisation**—or "institutionalised standardisation" as Milroy (2001, 542) calls it—**as an official imposition of "uniformity of usage" on various forms of the language** (Milroy 2001, 533–34). It is important to recognise that while such institutionalisation can be wide-reaching, as in government administration or the school system, it can also be limited to a single work with limited circulation. Note that the codification of grammar in a book, for example, irrespective of the size of the readership, entails a sort of institutionalisation. Grammar is, after all, a sort of institution in itself. Not only does the codification of grammar set out rules and standards for a particular language, but it also demarcates a particular variety of the language itself, thus establishing the language *qua* language and limiting the degree of permissible diversity, fluidity, and malleability of form.

2.1.8. Historicisation

As hinted at above, **historicisation is one of the key components in legitimising a particular form of the language.** Although all forms of a language—various dialects, the colloquial form, the prestige form, etc.—generally have their own long histories in one way or another, standard language cultures often present only the canonical form as having a long, storied, pure, unbroken, and thus authoritative history. Other forms of the language are commonly regarded as degenerate imitations of the standard form. Influence from other languages can often be regarded as contributing to the deterioration of the standard. When there is a dispute about whether a current linguistic form is 'correct' or 'incorrect', grammarians often appeal to historical corpora to justify their claim that a certain form is 'correct' over against another. Further, there is often a misguided apprehension that the ancient form of the language and the modern language either *are* the same or *should be* the same (Milroy 1999; Milroy 2001, 547–50).

2.2. Enregisterment and Transference

If up to this point we have outlined trends of standard language cultures in operation, we must now also consider what forces, circumstances, and societal developments lead to a particular form of the language being regarded as the 'prestige', 'canonical', and/or 'standard' variety in the first place. After all, the presence of a standard language implies the pre-existence of certain historical and cultural developments—and similar ongoing processes—that serve to index certain linguistic forms as 'standard' or 'prestigious' in the society.

In recent decades, linguistic anthropologists have developed a framework, known as *enregisterment*, for explaining how various social meanings (e.g., prestige) come to be associated with various linguistic forms and choices. Sets of such linguistic choices are what may be understood as language varieties. Central to this framework is the concept of indexicality. When a sign—a linguistic form, a gesture, a particular appearance, etc.—co-occurs with its meaning, it is considered indexical. Johnstone (2016, 633) cites as an analogy the sound of thunder, which, because it typically co-occurs with a storm in the physical world, can be used by itself to conjur the idea of a storm in a staged play. In a similar way, the use of certain linguistic forms—whether a specific word or pronunciation—due to their regular or frequent occurrence in particular social contexts, may evoke (or establish) a social identity by itself. *Enregisterment* thus refers to the processes by which certain performable (linguistic) signs come to be identified and grouped with registers that are imbued with social meaning. Agha (2003, 231) defines *enregisterment* as the "processes through which a linguistic repertoire becomes differentiable within a language as a socially recognized register of forms" (Silverstein 1993; Silverstein 2003; Agha 2003; Agha 2007; Johnstone 2016).

There are a number of cases in which the processes or consequences of enregisterment are relatively obvious, even for the non-specialist. Perhaps the clearest examples of enregisterment concern speech patterns associated with specific locales. While a full set of phonological features associated with a region constitute what may be referred to colloquially as an 'accent'—note the Cockney accent in the UK or the Boston accent in the USA—sometimes a single feature (or even lexeme) can enregister a regional or social identity. In Jordan, for example, pronouncing the Arabic letter ق as [g] is a characteristic of residents of Zarqa. Similarly, the use of the second-person plural pronoun *yunz* or *yinz* is characteristic of the variety of English spoken in Pittsburgh. Presumably, one conversation (or performance) at a time, hearers encounter these features in speakers associated (via various other social clues) with these locales. As a result, the linguistic features themselves come to take on the social values and traits of those who carry them (Agha 2003; Johnstone 2016).

Sometimes, however, there can be an intersection of social associations that lead to multiple possible avenues of enregisterment. For example, while the Cockney accent is regionally associated with East London, it also carries class undertones in that it is considered a working-class accent. Similarly, while pronouncing the Arabic letter ق as [g] may simply indicate that one is a resident of Zarqa, residents of Amman that pronounce ق as [g] may sound more masculine (and less urban) in that context, where most pronounce ق as the glottal stop [ʔ]. Depending on the range of social clues in any given situation, then, one hearing these features may enregister them by region, ethnicity, class, social status, wealth, educational background, or even by various personality traits of the speaker. Various linguistic signs can also be enregistered to specific (and limited) times, settings, or activities. In many cases, two people hearing the same speaker—depending on their own background and experience—may enregister the linguistic signs differently. It is thus not difficult to imagine how the dynamicity of social clues can result in the intersection of several possible targets of enregisterment. This also underscores how enregisterment is a constantly ongoing and dynamic process; it is never static (Agha 2003; Johnstone 2016).

Moreoever, though we might not think of it at first, even the opposition between 'correct' and 'incorrect' is enregistered to a degree, which plays into the concept of a standard language ideology. Widespread ideas about how language works, such as the belief that non-standard speech is not just different but actually 'incorrect', can determine how distinct varieties are enregistered, which has significant ideological implications for how speakers of non-standard varieties are regarded in the society. For those who hold such a belief, a non-standard linguistic sign might simply be enregistered as 'wrong'. This, in turn, can lead to a disparaging view of speakers of certain varieties. Note, for example, how many English speakers are quick to deride [ˈæks] as an 'incorrect' pronunciation of the word *ask*. For those without such a belief about non-standard language, however, the same sign is likely to be enregistered with greater sensitivity to the social background of the speaker, whether regional, ethnic, urban vs suburban, etc. (Johnstone 2016, 639).

While the examples cited above illustrate what happens during the process of enregisterment on a granular level, such interactions must occur countless times for the enregistered varieties—i.e., language 'registers'—to be recognised throughout the society. Integral to this wide-scale social transmission of cultural values embedded in language, which occurs one speech event or message at a time, are the sociohistorical processes of valorisation and circulation. Valorisation may be regarded as the association of some societal value with certain linguistic signs and/or language varieties. Circulation, on the other hand, involves the widespread dissemination of certain cultural values embedded in these language varieties. Both valorisation and circulation are necessary for a particular variety to be widely regarded as the 'standard' or 'prestige' form of the language (Agha 2003, 231–32, 243, 246–47, 264, 270).

For Agha, one of the principle sociohistorical practices involved in the process of enregisterment (of a particular variety as the 'standard' or 'prestige' form of the language) consists of certain linguistic forms being perceptually associated with certain 'exemplary speakers'. Such exemplary speakers can be language teachers in schools, invented characters in literary works, famous people in society, or even popular figures from history. As various linguistic signs come to be associated with certain exemplary speakers, the societal values associated with the speakers gradually (and subtly) come to be transferred to the particular form of the language itself. Certain linguistic registers thus come to have social currency and developing proficiency in these registers is incentivised. In this way, we may speak of the 'valorisation' of certain registers (Agha 2003, 251–52).

In some cases, however, such valorisation may initially be restricted to a limited 'audience' of grammarians or language enthusiasts. For such registers to be widely recognised as 'prestigious' or 'standard', linguistic materials and behaviour that further such sociolinguistic associations must undergo wide circulation. For Agha (2003, 246–47), as noted above, the social transmission of cultural values embedded in language occurs one speech event or message at a time. This can occur in casual conversation, public speeches, formal instruction, popular media, or even in written discourse. In all of these contexts, the cultural values associated with certain forms of the language must be reinforced by those associated with the speaker or author of the message. In many cases, however, the social transformation of a particular register into a widely recognised 'standard' is mediated by widely circulated genres of metadiscourse. This may involve certain prescriptivist features of a more specialist work (e.g., grammatical treatise) being popularised in a more accessible or widely circulated genre, such as a novel or a popular handbook (Agha 2003, 251–52). Public performances characterised by certain linguistic forms can also serve the process of circulation.

Over time, all these processes can work together to transform and entrench a particular form or register of a language into the 'standard' canonical form in the society. If this is the case, then the existence of a standard language culture in a given society implies that a series of significant sociohistorical developments have already taken place. As such, identifying a standard language culture can be just as illuminating for sociohistorical purposes as for linguistic ones.

Nevertheless, despite the clear value that the theoretical framework of enregisterment has for linguistic anthropology and sociolinguistics, one wonders how applicable it is to the data to which we have access from the medieval grammarians. After all, for most linguistic anthropologists and sociolinguists, the process of enregisterment necessarily involves performances (or speech events) encountered in real time, so that linguistic signs (and language varieties) can gradually become associated with social types. Because of the chronological gap between us and the object of study of the present work—not to mention the limited data we have from the period—it is difficult or even impossible to access the societal values associated with the speakers or the social contexts in which the link between form and type was made. Theorising about such societal values and social contexts is bound to result in at least some speculative reconstruction.

Nevertheless, while we must admit that we cannot apply this theoretical framework to the medieval grammarians in precisely the same way (or with the same degree of certainty) as linguistic anthropologists do for modern languages, it may serve as a helpful heuristic. After all, we do have some societal values associated with linguistic form communicated to us through the writings of the grammarians. In other cases, they may be only implied. In either case, even if we do not have access to the real-time performances and speech events through which processes of enregisterment undoubtedly occurred during the medieval period, the consequences thereof are likely refracted throughout the texts we have at our disposal. Moreover, it is likely that some of the processes of enregisterment were based in textual artefacts themselves. As we will see, because the 'standard' language championed by the grammarians was closely associated with written corpora of 'ancient' times, their readers would have had to imagine or envision the original social types associated with the linguistic register. In this respect, our vantage point is perhaps closer to their perspective than the chronological gap might otherwise entail. Therefore, even though it involves some degree of speculation, applying the theoretical framework of enregisterment may serve as a helpful heuristic for at least parts of our analysis. The potential insight is worth the speculation, especially considering the fact that the overall argument of the book would likely be unaffected if our utilisation of the framework of enregisterment is found to be inapplicable.

Moreover, for our own specific purposes here, we might also expand on the work of linguistic anthropologists with respect to enregisterment. While the process of enregisterment is often described as happening in the context of real-time 'live' performances and speech events, we might suggest that a wider phenomenon of *transference* might help explain certain data points for which access to real-time speech events is not possible. In the present work, we will use the term 'transference' to refer to cases in which the social types associated with certain linguistic signs are shifted to other social reference points that may be thought to co-occur with those same signs. A clear example of this phenomenon would be how a particular language variety associated with a limited group of speakers comes to be associated with a much wider demographic of which they are a part. In many cases, this is due to the fact that those outside of the group and the wider demographic might have much more exposure to the limited group, which they might mistakenly perceive as representative of the wider demographic.

An example of this phenomenon in modern times may be found in how those who have never been to the United States might misunderstand the linguistic portrayal of certain groups in media or film as generally representative or even characteristic of a much wider demographic to which they belong. A similar phenomenon likely occurred in medieval times, largely due to the fact that members of society might only have had limited access (e.g., through the written text) to certain groups. Naturally, this phenomenon is especially applicable when looking to the past for linguistic exemplars. This concept will feature prominently later in the book as we consider how both 'ancient' and contemporary sources of the standard language were viewed and described by the medieval grammarians.

3.0. Language Ideology and Performance

In cultures with a standard language ideology, there is often a high premium placed on 'performance' of the standard canonical language in various societal contexts. While 'performance' can have a variety of connotations, it may be defined, in a linguistic context at least, as "verbal art" or a "mode of speaking" that often occurs in a specific setting in which at least one speaker or performer is elevated (Bauman 1975, 290). Performance is often accompanied by a number of distinct features that set it apart from normal speech (Bauman 1975; Bell and Gibson 2011).

In terms of language, speakers (or performers) tend to make use of an array of linguistic features distinct from those at play in other contexts, such as everyday conversation. This is particularly common at the beginning of a discourse, during which archaic codes or opening formulae may clue the audience in to the fact that a performance is coming. In certain ritual or liturgical contexts, a performance can only be validated if the speaker performs certain clear and prerequisite signals. Beyond opening formulae and ritual signals, a performance mode of speaking may also be characterised by other grammatical and stylistic features such as metaphor, rhyme, vowel harmony, and parallelism. Modifications to speed of speech, pitch, voice quality, and vocalisation may also go along with performance (Bauman 1975; Bell and Gibson 2011). Generally speaking, performance modes of speaking are also frequently characterised by "exaggerated linguistic forms" (Bell and Gibson 2011, 558).

As such, a performance mode of speaking should not be regarded as a unidirectional activity. It also requires an audience keenly aware of the expectations associated with a particular performance. By engaging in performance, the speaker (or performer) submits themselves to be held accountable by the audience. The audience, in turn, evaluates their performance to make sure it meets the criteria afforded by the context. The performer is expected to display linguistic and rhetorical proficiency in their communiciation. This mutual understanding leads to a highly charged situation in which the performer strives to show utmost linguistic ability, on the one hand, and the audience endeavours to subject them to increased scrutiny, on the other. If the performer succeeds in meeting the expectations of the audience, they may achieve a higher status in the society, even if only temporarily. Failing to meet the expectations of the audience, however, can turn the performer into an object of ridicule (Bauman 1975; Bell and Gibson 2011).

While the term 'performance' might drum up images from the sphere of the theatre for us as moderns, it actually encompasses a wide variety of settings and activities. Public speeches, recitation of poetry, sermons, prayers, and chanting a sacred text in a religious context are all examples where these principles apply. This is especially important to remember as we consider performance in medieval Jewish and Muslim contexts.

Although many of the features of performance apply in a relatively localised context, its cumulative impact on society should not be minimised. Drawing on some of the principles outlined above (see §2.0), we may call attention to the fact that performance as a societal phenomenon is a prime candidate for reinforcing the cultural values associated with certain linguistic registers. Because prestige and status may be conferred on successful and accomplished performers, it is one of the most significant participants in the processes of valorisation and—assuming it is popular—circulation of certain cultural values embedded in certain types of language. In this way, it helps shape the language ideology of the society at large, one performance at a time.

4.0. Conclusions

The relevance of these topics for the Hebrew and Arabic grammatical traditions of the Middle Ages will become more and more apparent as we proceed through the primary material in the remainder of this book. What is worth reiterating here, however, is that, when dealing with language ideology, the object of study is not the language itself, at least not first and foremost. Rather, a language ideology framework is concerned primarily with language users' *beliefs and attitudes* regarding their languages and the languages of others.

As such—and this is the critical point—describing the language ideology of a given individual or community is unlikely to produce an account that accurately maps onto the facts on the ground. In fact, it is quite common to find that the beliefs and attitudes of language users are often in conflict with actual language practice as analysed by more objective metrics. A clear example of such would be how many native Arabic speakers today believe that Classical Arabic and Modern Standard Arabic are essentially the same entity. In reality, there are differences in phonology, morphology, syntax, and lexicon.[9] Note, for example, how the specific phonological features of CA or MSA exhibit variation according to the regional dialects of the readers and/or local pronunciation traditions. Similarly, we might also mention how there is a belief among many Arabic speakers that when two Arabs from different regions meet, they speak in Modern Standard Arabic for the sake of mutual intelligibility. In actuality, such meetings generally result in a somewhat elevated or accommodating version of dialectal Arabic rather than full-on Modern Standard Arabic. Finally, there are more subjective or aesthetic beliefs about language—for example, that the language of the *Qur'ān* is insurpassable in beauty—that are not necessarily possible to prove one way or another.

All of this underscores the importance of realising that an analysis of language ideology should not be mistaken for an analysis of language. As we proceed through the primary material in

---

[9] The differences between CA and MSA may, however, be exaggerated by some scholars. Note that MSA is much more narrowly and prescriptively defined than CA. This is especially the case in syntax. The lexicon of MSA has also expanded to cope with modern terminology, new contexts of use, etc.

the remainder of this book, then, we may find that the language ideology of the grammarians paints a picture at odds with what is known about Hebrew and Arabic of the Middle Ages from other sources. This should be regarded as a feature, rather than a bug, of this approach. When what people believe about language is in conflict with actual linguistic practice 'on the ground', we can learn much about the sociolinguistic and sociohistorical contexts in which both the ideology and the practice coexisted.

4. DEFINING THE STANDARD LANGUAGE AND ITS CORPUS

As we have seen, language ideology is a cluster of beliefs and attitudes about language that are often expressed indirectly, and that we may perceive through an examination of the assumptions underlying the expressions of an individual or a community. Such assumptions are not merely an ancillary issue, but rather undergird the codification of the grammar of a language and thus inform how the entire work is carried out. They help explain not only why a particular form of language was chosen to be codified as the 'standard', but also what sort of criteria determine authentic examples of the standard language. Understanding the language ideology behind the codification of a language's grammar is thus illuminating for understanding both early conceptions of the language and the status of that language in its society and culture through history. As such, language ideology is of utmost relevance for understanding the work of the medieval Hebrew and Arabic grammarians.

What is more, because language ideologies are cultural entities, they are transferable and susceptible to influence among members of a particular society. As we will demonstrate in the remainder of this book, the language ideologies current among the medieval Hebrew grammarians were markedly similar to those of their Arabic counterparts. While such lines of similarity may have come about in a variety of ways—direct influence, wider shared culture, etc.—simply identifying and establishing a

 https://doi.org/10.11647/OBP.0382.04

number of shared features of (standard) language ideology in these two traditions constitutes a worthy avenue of inquiry in its own right.

In the present and following chapter, then, we will survey six features of shared (standard) language ideology that appear to be attested in both the Hebrew grammarians and the Arabic grammarians of the ʿAbbasid period (750–1258 CE). Because the first three similarities are more closely associated with the nature of the standard language and its corpus (see §§1.0–3.0 in the present chapter), whereas the latter three similarities touch on the grammarians' goals for the standard language (see chapter 5, §§1.0–3.0), our analysis of the primary material is split into two chapters consistent with these themes in order to facilitate organisation for the reader. Nevertheless, all aspects of language ideology treated in both chapters are closely interrelated and overlap considerably. Naturally, the theoretical considerations outlined earlier (see chapter 3) will serve as the framework through which we will analyse the primary material.

As we proceed through each feature, we will begin with an overview of the data from the medieval Hebrew grammarians who wrote in Judeo-Arabic (specifically during the ʿAbbasid period) before turning to the Arabic grammarians for the sake of comparison. Because this book is primarily focused on the medieval Hebrew grammarians who wrote in Judeo-Arabic, sections on the Arabic grammarians will be somewhat abbreviated, including only a selection of relevant grammarians and often drawing on secondary literature where possible to call attention to parallels in the traditions.[10]

While these chapters are primarily focused on presenting the primary data to identify and establish shared features of standard language ideology, we will return to discuss possible explanations for such similarity at the close of the book (see chapter 6). As we have already hinted at, an ideological analysis of *lughat al-ʿibrāniyyīn* 'the language of the Hebrews' will suggest that elements of the Arabic grammatical tradition absorbed into the Hebrew grammatical tradition of the ʿAbbasid period include not only terms and concepts but cultural elements and language ideologies as well. In particular, both traditions appear to reflect significant traits of a standard language ideology as outlined earlier, each of which we will examine in turn below.

1.0. Cultural Possession: لغة العبرانيين

Much of our contemporary understanding of what language is we take for granted. While modern nomenclature tends to treat language as an abstract entity (e.g., Spanish, English, French), this was not necessarily the case among the medieval grammarians. While more abstract terms like אלעבראני (≈ العبراني) 'Hebrew (ms)' or אלעבראניה (≈ العبرانية) 'Hebrew (fs)' and العربية 'Arabic' are used to refer to the languages, we also find nomenclature that specifically references the speakers of the language, such as לֻגָה בני

[10] Much of the analysis of the standard language ideology of the Arabic grammarians is based on the work of Brustad (2010; 2016; 2017).

לגֿה אסראיל (≈ لغة بني إسرائيل) 'the language of the Israelites' and לגֿה אלעבראניין (≈ لغة العبرانيين) 'the language of the Hebrews' among the Hebrew grammarians and لسان العرب 'the language of the Arabs' and كلام العرب 'the speech/idiom of the Arabs' among the Arabic grammarians.[11] Although these terms have slightly different nuances—which we will deal with progressively throughout the book—they all construe the language as belonging to its speakers. As such, these terms may reflect a language ideology that regarded Hebrew and Arabic as cultural possessions of their respective communities of speakers. We will address this idea in greater detail as we proceed through the primary data below.

1.1. Hebrew Grammarians

The idea that Hebrew is a language belonging to its speakers appears to be evidenced in a number of early grammarians.

1.1.1. Saadia Gaon (882–942 CE)

There are a number of such examples in the writings of Saadia Gaon (882–942 CE), a well-known Hebrew grammarian of the Middle Ages from the Fayyūm in Upper Egypt.[12] In the first place, although Saadia's grammar is commonly referred to as כתב אללגֿה (≈ كتب اللغة) 'The Books of Language', he also calls it כתאב פציח

[11] For more on the nomenclature of Hebrew and Arabic, see Maman (2004, 53–55). Note, however, that terms like *kalām al-ʿarab* and *al-ʿarabiyya* are more nuanced and require further explanation. We will return to this topic in greater detail later in the book.

[12] For more on Saadia's life, see Malter (1921, 25–26).

לגה̈ אלעבראניין (≈ كتاب فصيح لغة العبرانيين) ‘The Book of the Eloquence of the Language of the Hebrews’ (Skoss 1952a, 283, 290–91). Indeed, early on in his section on the vowels, Saadia discusses features that יכ̇ץ̈ לגה̈ אלעבראניין (≈ يخصّ لغة العبرانيين) ‘are particular to the language of the Hebrews’ (Skoss 1952a, 290–91). A similar phrase is found in *Sefer Ha-Galuy*, in which Saadia states that he composed his book לתצחיח אעראב לגה̈ אלעבראניין (≈ لتصحيح إعراب لغة العبرانيين) ‘for correcting the *iʿrāb* of the language of the Hebrews’ (Harkavy 1891, 499; Malter 1913, 157).

That Saadia regarded the Hebrew language as a cultural possession (see chapter 3, §2.1.1) is made further explicit by his statements in *Sefer Ha-Egron.*[13] Following an Arabic introduction, the main Hebrew section of *Sefer Ha-Egron* begins by recounting the history of the Hebrew language from the creation of the world. At first, there was only one holy language in the world, but when the earth was split, the number of languages multiplied according to the number of peoples. At this point, Saadia states that לֹא נִשְׁאַר לְשׁוֹן הַקּוֹדֶשׁ רַק בְּפִי בְנֵי עֵבֶר לְבַדָּם (*lō nišʾar lšōn haqqoḏɛš raq bfī vnē ʿɛvɛr lvaddɔ̄m*) ‘the holy language remained in the mouths of none other than the sons of ʿEber’ (Harkavy 1891, 499), essentially saying that it became the sole possession of the Hebrews. In *Sefer Ha-Galuy*, Saadia also states that the nation has forgotten לגתהא אלפציחה̈ וכלאמהא אלבדיע (≈ لغتها الفصيحة وكلامها

[13] For background on *Sefer Ha-Egron*, see Harkavy (1891, 1–39) and Malter (1921, 138–39).

البديع) ‘*their* clear language and *their* wonderful idiom’ (for more on this full passage, see chapter 5, §3.1.1).

1.1.2. Judah ben David Ḥayyūj (945–1000 CE)

Judah ben David Ḥayyūj (945–1000 CE), a Hebrew grammarian from Morocco but active in al-Andalus (i.e., Spain), exhibits similar nomenclature when discussing Hebrew. When addressing various grammatical features of Biblical Hebrew, he describes them with reference to the linguistic practice of *al-ʿibrāniyyūn* ‘the Hebrews’. For example, when discussing the syllable structure of Biblical Hebrew, he writes the following in his book on weak verbal roots known as *Kitāb al-afʿāl ḏawāt ḥurūf al-līn* (Jastrow 1897, 5):

> واقول أنّ العبرانيين لا يبدون بساكن ولا يقفون على متحرّك ولا يكون عندهم ساكن او ساكنان ملتقيان إلّا بعد متحرّك متقدّم[14]
>
> And I say that the Hebrews do not begin [a word] with a silent *shewa*, nor do they end a word with a mobile *shewa*.

---

[14] The reader may notice occasional ‘non-standard’ orthographical forms in various Arabic passages quoted throughout this book, such as اقول or او without a *hamzah*. This is especially the case with Judeo-Arabic texts. Rather than regularising these—thus reinforcing the standard language ideology in modern scholarship—we have merely replicated what is present in each text edition we have utilised. This applies to all passages quoted throughout the book and readers should consult the original editions to get an idea of the orthographic conventions utilised therein.

> And they do not have silent *shewa* or two consecutive cases of silent *shewa* except after a preceding vowel.

It is significant to note that, for Ḥayyūj, these features of the Tiberian vocalisation tradition of Biblical Hebrew are described as reflecting the linguistic practice and speech patterns of *al-ʿibrāniyyūn* 'the Hebrews'. It is not *the Hebrew text* that disallows a word beginning with a consonant with silent *shewa* but rather *the Hebrews themselves* who do not speak this way.

A similar conceptualisation of *al-ʿibrāniyyūn* 'the Hebrews' is found elsewhere in Ḥayyūj in another discussion of syllable structure (*Kitāb al-afʿāl ḏawāt ḥurūf al-līn*; Jastrow 1897, 7):

> واقول ايضا أنّ العبرانيين لا يجمعون بين ساكنَيْنِ غيرِ لينين إلّا فى الوقف وأنقطاعِ الكلام... وحركتُها فى جلّ كلامهم على تلك الشروط اللتي قدّمت

> And I also say that the Hebrews do not make two non-weak consonants vocalised with silent *shewa* adjacent to one another except in pause and at the cutting off of speech... and its vowel in the majority of their speech (*kalām*) is according to those conditions that I outlined earlier...

Once again, features of the Tiberian vocalisation tradition and its oral reading are described as reflecting the linguistic practice and speech patterns of *al-ʿibrāniyyūn* 'the Hebrews'.

1.1.3. Jonah ibn Janāḥ (ca 990–ca 1050 CE)

Jonah ibn Janāḥ (ca 990–ca 1050 CE), a Hebrew grammarian from al-Andalus, also uses similar phrases when discussing Hebrew grammar. When explaining his methodology, he writes the following in his book on Hebrew roots entitled *Kitāb al-uṣūl* (Neubauer 1968, 13):

واذا رأيتنى اكثر من تكرير لفظة ما اسما كانت او فعلا مما كان يمكن ان يستغنى ببعض ما اذكر منها عن الجميع. فانّى انما افعل ذلك لاظهر وجوه استعمال العبرانيين لتلك اللفظة فى مواضع مختلفة

> And if you notice that I repeat a word, whether a noun or a verb, when it was possible to manage with just one of its [forms] that I mention [and to dispense with] all [of the rest], I do this to show the various ways that the Hebrews use (*istiʿmāl al-ʿibrāniyyīn*) this word in different places.

The key phrase in this passage is استعمال العبرانيين 'the usage of the Hebrews', which once again refers to the linguistic practice of speakers or language users.

1.1.4. Abū al-Faraj Hārūn ibn al-Faraj (first half of 11th c. CE)

Abū al-Faraj Hārūn (first half of 11th c. CE), a Karaite Hebrew grammarian of Jerusalem, also associates Biblical Hebrew grammar with the linguistic practice of speakers. At the beginning of his chapter פי אקסאם אלכלאם (≈ في أقسام الكلام) 'on the components of speech' in his book *al-Kitāb al-kāfī fī al-lugha al-ʿibrāniyya* (I.2.1), he writes the following (Khan et al. 2003):

אלכלאם אלמסתעמל תלתה אקסאם אסםٌ ופעْלٌ וחרף יסמיה אלדקדוקיון כאדמא[15]

> Natural speech (*al-kalām al-mustaʿmal*; lit.: 'speech in use') has three parts: the noun, the verb, and what the grammarians have referred to as a 'serving' element (*ḫādim*).

---

[15] ≈ الكلام المستعمل ثلاثة أقسام اسمٌ وَفِعْلٌ وحرف يسميه الدقدوقيون خادما.

The particular phrase אלכלאם אלמסתעמל (≈ الكلام المستعمل) 'speech in use', which envisions some type of actual linguistic practice, is reminiscent of Ibn Janāḥ's phrase استعمال العبرانيين 'the usage of the Hebrews' mentioned above.

Elsewhere in this work, Abū al-Faraj refers specifically to the linguistic practice of *al-ʿibrāniyyūn*. When discussing the conjoining of a noun to a verb (I.4.7), he writes the following (Khan et al. 2003):

> פיגוז אסתעמאל אלעבראניין איצׄא מא הדא סבילה פי אצׄאפה אלזמאן אלי אלפעל[16]
>
> So it is permissible for the Hebrews to use (*istiʿmāl al-ʿibrāniyyīn*) the conjoining of a temporal phrase to a verb in the same way.

Also, when discussing the role of a preformative *mem* in passive participles (I.27.52), he writes the following (Khan et al. 2003):

> פלא ימתנע אן יכון אלעבראניון אדכלו אלמים עלי אלמאצׄי מנה ולם ידכלוהא עלי פעל מא יסמא פאעלה ללאמרין אלדין אפתרקא פיהמא[17]
>
> It is not implausible that the Hebrews attached *mem* to the past-tense form of the verb but did not attach it to a verb whose agent is mentioned, on account of the two features with respect to which they differ.

In each of these examples, the language of Biblical Hebrew is ascribed to the real linguistic usage and practice of *al-ʿibrāniyyūn*.

---

[16] ≈ فيجوز استعمال العبرانيين أيضا ما هذا سبيله في إضافة الزمان إلى الفعل.

[17] ≈ فلا يمتنع أن يكون العبرانيون أدخلوا الميم على الماضي منه ولم يدخلوها على فعل ما يسمى فاعله للأمرين الذين افترقا فيهما.

1.2. Comparison with the Arabic Tradition

Nomenclature referring to the Arabic language specifically with reference to its community of speakers is also attested in the Arabic grammarians.

1.2.1. al-Khalīl ibn Aḥmad (d. 786/791 CE)

Al-Khalīl ibn Aḥmad (d. 786/791 CE), the famous grammarian and lexicographer of Baṣra, describes Arabic in a similar way. When explaining morphological variation in verbal forms of the root *n-y-ʾ* in his dictionary *Kitāb al-ʿayn* (8.392; al-Makhzūmī and al-Sāmarrāʾī 1989), he writes the following:

> وأنأتُ اللّحم إناءةً إذا لم تنضجه، ولكنّ العرب إذا أرادت أن تَسْتعملَ الهاءَ في هذا المعنى قالت: أنهأتُ اللّحم إنهاءً
>
> And [you say] 'I insufficiently cooked (*anaʾtu... ināʾat-an*) the meat' if you did not cook it thoroughly. But the Arabs, if they want to use (*tastaʿmila*) the *hāʾ* with this meaning, say 'I insufficiently cooked (*anhaʾtu... inhāʾ-an*) the meat'.

In addition to the Arabs' usage of the language, there are also certain pronouncements about what is permissible in the 'speech of the Arabs', as in the following (2.348):

> ولم يأتِ شيءٌ من كلام العرب يَزيدُ على خمسة أحرف إلا أن تلحقها زيادات ليست من أصلها أو يُوَصَلَ حكايةً يُحكى بها، كقول الشاعر: فَتَفْتَحُه طَوْراً وطَوراً تُجيفُه فتَسمعُ في الحالَيْنِ منه جَلَنبَلَقْ. يَحكي صوتَ بابٍ في فَتْحِهِ وإصفاقه
>
> There are no [words] that occur in the speech of the Arabs (*kalām al-ʿarab*) that exceed five letters except when addi-

> tions not belonging to the root (i.e., prefixes, suffixes, enclitics) are attached to it or when it is onomatopoeic, as in the saying of the poet, "Whether you open it one time or you close it one time, in either case, you will hear [the sound] *jalanbalaq*," which is onomatopoeic for the sound of a door when it is opened or closed.

In this passage, a principle of word formation in Arabic is described as reflecting *kalām al-ʿarab* 'the speech of the Arabs'. Interestingly, a poetic verse is cited to provide an example. We will return to the significance of this in a later section (see §2.0).

1.2.2. Sībawayh (d. ca 796 CE)

Sībawayh (d. ca 796 CE), the famous Persian grammarian of Arabic from Shiraz, exhibits similar wording about the language usage of the Arabs. After citing a number of examples to illustrate a point, Sībawayh concludes by saying (1.165; Haroun 1988):

واعلم أنَّ العرب يَستخفّون فيحذفون التنوينَ والنون، ولا يَتغيّرُ من المعنى

> Note that the Arabs make light and omit *tanwīn* and *nūn* and the meaning is not changed.

Elsewhere in his grammar, when discussing the realisation of a sequence of *hamzahs*, he writes the following (3.549; Haroun 1988):

فليس من كلام العرب أن تَلتقي همزتان فتُحقّقا، ومن كلام العرب تخفيفُ الأولى وتحقيقُ الآخِرة

> And it is not part of the speech of the Arabs (*kalām al-ʿarab*) for two *hamzahs* to meet and be realised. But what is part of the speech of the Arabs (*kalām al-ʿarab*) is for the first to be elided and the second to be realised.

As in the above example, Sībawayh appeals to the linguistic practice and speech patterns of *al-ʿarab* 'the Arabs' to explain various grammatical features. As in al-Khalīl's *Kitāb al-ʿayn*, the phrase used is *kalām al-ʿarab* 'the speech of the Arabs'.

Sībawayh elsewhere notes that, as a principle, what is permissible in the language should be based on the usage of the Arabs (1.414; Haroun 1988; Marogy 2010b, 59):

فاستَعملْ من هذا ما استَعملتِ العربُ، وأَجِزْ منه ما أجازوا

> And use (*fa-staʿmil*) from this what the Arabs use (*istaʿmalat*), and allow from it what they allow.

Once again, this demonstrates that Sībawayh regarded the language as strongly associated with—or perhaps even a possession of—its speakers, namely *al-ʿarab* 'the Arabs'.

1.2.3. al-Farrāʾ (d. 822/823 CE)

The same type of language continues in slightly later grammarians as well, such as the esteemed Kūfan grammarian al-Farrāʾ (d. 822/823 CE). In his *Maʿānī al-qurʾān* (3.260; Najātī and al-Najjār 1955), when discussing various readers' pronunciations of the word يَسْرِ 'passes', he writes the following:

«واللَّيْلِ إذَا يَسْرِ»... وقد قرأ القراء: «يَسرى» بإثبات الياءِ، و«يسر» بحذفها، وحذفها أحب إلىّ لمشاكلتها رءوس الآيات، ولأن العرب قد تحذف الياء، وتكتفى بكسر ما قبلها منها، أنشدنى بعضهم. كفّاكَ كفٌّ ما تُلِيقُ دِرْهَماً جوداً، وأخرى تُعطِ بالسيف الدِّما

> "And by night, when it passes (*yasri/yasrī*)" (Al-Fajr [89.4])... while some readers read this word as *yasrī* with a clear *yāʾ*, others read it as *yasr(i)* with omission of *yāʾ*. Its

> omission is preferable to me, due to it being more suitable to the final word of a verse, and because the Arabs (*al-ʿarab*) might omit the *yāʾ* but still be content with pronouncing [the letter] that precedes it with *kasra*. One of [the Arabs] has recited the following line of poetry to me: "Your hands—one spares a *dirham* generously, but the other gives (*tuʿṭi/tuʿṭī*) blood with the sword."

In this case, the omission of a word-final vowel letter *yāʾ*—and pronouncing *kasra* on the preceding letter—is regarded as an example of the linguistic practice of the Arabs. The significance of quoting poetry to exemplify the grammatical phenomenon is a topic to which we will return in the following section (§2.2.2).

As we might expect, the phrase *kalām al-ʿarab* also features prominently in al-Farrāʾ, as in the following passage discussing the use of plural verbs with a singular subject (3.42; Najātī and al-Najjār 1955):

> فى كثير من كلام العرب، أن تجمع العرب فعل الواحد، منه قول الله عز وجل: «قَالَ رَبِّ ارْجِعونِ»
>
> It is common in the speech of the Arabs (*kalām al-ʿarab*) for the Arabs to make the verb of a singular [agent] plural, as in the statement of God Almighty, "He says, 'Lord, let me come back!'" (Al-Muʾminun 23.99).

Similarly, the morphosyntactic features of the *Qurʾān* are described as reflecting the linguistic practice of the Arabs and consistent with most of the speech of the Arabs (*kalām al-ʿarab*).

1.2.4. Ibn al-Sarrāj (d. 928/929 CE)

Abū Bakr Muḥammad ibn al-Sarrāj (d. 928/929 CE), an Arabic grammarian of Baghdad, reflects similar conceptions of language usage in his *Kitāb al-uṣūl fī al-naḥw*. Note the following comment about the usage of the conjunction/particle *wāw* (1.420; Fatlī 1996):

واعلم: أنّ العربَ تستعملُ الواوَ مبتدأة بمعنى: «رُبَّ» فيقولون: وبلد قطعتُ، يريدونَ ورُبَّ بلد وهذا كثير

> And know that the Arabs use (*tastaʿmilu*) *wāw* as a subject with the meaning 'few/much (*rubba*)'. So when they say, 'And the country (*wa-balad*) have I cut off', they actually mean '(And) much of the country (*wa-rubba balad*)', and this is frequent.

The use of the particle *wāw* in this way is described as reflecting the speech patterns of the Arabs. In this context, it is particularly noteworthy that the intention of the speakers (i.e., يريدون 'they intend [the meaning]') is considered in relation to usage.

1.3. Analysis

Although it may seem like a minor point, it is important to recognise that language was inextricably linked to those who spoke it for both the Hebrew and Arabic grammarians of the ʿAbbasid period. As we have seen at least in the writings of Saadia, this may have indicated that, ideologically, the language was regarded as a cultural possession of its speakers. This would be in line with certain features of a standard language ideology outlined earlier (see chapter 3, §2.1.1). And yet, the language-as-a-cultural-possession ideology is often accompanied by a belief that the standard language is not innate in native speakers of contemporary society but must be learned. Indeed, the canonical form of the language is regarded as existing beyond the members of the society (Milroy 2001, 537–38).

At first glance, then, ascribing such an ideology to the medieval Hebrew and Arabic grammarians would seem to conflict with their referencing actual linguistic practice of speakers in their grammatical descriptions. Such a tension, however, is predicated on certain assumptions about what the Hebrew grammarians meant by *al-ʿibrāniyyūn* 'the Hebrews', on the one hand, and what the Arabic grammarians meant by *al-ʿarab* 'the Arabs' or *kalām al-ʿarab* 'the speech/idiom of the Arabs', on the other. As we will see in the following section, the referents of these terms—not necessarily the grammarians' contemporaries—are not always intuitive. When properly understood, they support ascribing a language-as-a-cultural-possession ideology to the medieval grammarians, and this within a wider framework of a robust standard language ideology.

2.0. Exemplary Ancient Speakers: العبرانيون القدماء الأولون

The preceding section left us with a question regarding the identity of *al-ʿibrāniyyūn* 'the Hebrews' and *al-ʿarab* 'the Arabs' in the works of the medieval grammarians. If these groups are considered exemplary speakers of their respective languages, then their specific identity is of utmost relevance for constructing the language ideology of the grammarians. The crux of the matter concerns whether the medieval grammarians regarded themselves, their contemporaries, and/or figures from the past as comprising the membership of such groups. What a careful analysis of these terms will show is that, in the case of both the Hebrew and Arabic grammarians, these terms refer to exemplary speakers from the past and not their contemporaries.[18] In each of the traditions, an ancient—and sacred—corpus of texts is what determines the 'correct' linguistic features of the canonical standard language. From the perspective of a standard language ideology, this is an important part of the language existing in an ideal form. Grammarians of each tradition, therefore, need to exercise discernment in determining which sources, traditions, examples, etc. from these corpora merit inclusion in their descriptions of the language.

2.1. Hebrew Grammarians

Among the Hebrew grammarians we find that the expression *al-ʿibrāniyyūn* 'the Hebrews' refers first and foremost to language users of the biblical period. Secondarily, however, it can also refer to those of the mishnaic period or even the *payṭanim* (i.e., Hebrew poets) of the Byzantine period.

2.1.1. Judah ben David Ḥayyūj (945–1000 CE)

Ḥayyūj, who was earlier quoted referring to the linguistic practices of *al-ʿibrāniyyūn* 'the Hebrews', supplies a most helpful comment on the matter in his *Kitāb al-afʿāl ḏawāt ḥurūf al-līn* (Jastrow 1897, 4):

والواجبُ علينا اهلِ الشوق الى هذه اللغة والتطلّع نحوها ان نقتدى فيها
بالعبرانيين القدماء الاوّلين الناشئين فيها المطبوعين عليها لا سيّما لغة الوحى

[18] This is another reason why it is important to identify the 'fieldwork' *topos* as ideological in nature (see §3.0).

> وكلام النّبوّة وأنْ نقفو فيها اثارهم ونسلك بها مسالكهم ونجريها على مناهجهم فاذا فعلْنا ذلك انبنى كلامنا على اساسه وتفرّع لنا من اصله وعَلِمْنَا من اللغة ما جهلناه وٱنتفعنا بما علمناه
>
> It is necessary for us, who are passionate for this language and aspire to it, to emulate in [how we use the language] the first ancient Hebrews who grew up in it and were naturally accustomed to it, especially with respect to the language of inspiration and prophetic speech. We should follow their footsteps in the language, walk in their paths with the language, and carry out the language according to their practices. If we do this, our speech (*kalām*) will be built upon its foundation and branch out from its root to us. We will learn what we had been ignorant of regarding the language and benefit from what we learn.

When Ḥayyūj refers to the linguistic practices of *al-ʿibrāniyyūn* 'the Hebrews', then, he is referring to those first ancient Hebrews (العبرانيون القدماء الأولون) who grew up (الناشئون) with the language and were naturally accustomed to it (المطبوعون عليها). In other words, *al-ʿibrāniyyūn* 'the Hebrews' are native speakers of Hebrew, but not of the contemporary period. As Maman (2004, 53) points out, the term refers to those speakers of Hebrew who lived in the biblical or mishnaic periods. It does not refer to their contemporaries or even themselves.

What is more, not only does this passage indicate that the term *al-ʿibrāniyyūn* 'the Hebrews' refers to those ancient speakers of Hebrew, but it also demonstrates that the linguistic practice of the ancients served as the standard according to which one ought to evaluate proper and improper Hebrew. Such a claim would seem obvious inasmuch as the linguistic practice of the ancients and Biblical Hebrew constitute two different ways of referring to the same thing. However, while generally true, this is not always the case.

There is no doubt that, when Ḥayyūj refers to how the Hebrews treat consonant clusters, he is basing his statements on the Tiberian vocalisation tradition of the Bible.[19] For him—at least in such instances—this was synonymous with the linguistic practice of the ancient Hebrews. In other words, the Hebrew found in the Bible—the Tiberian vocalisation of the Bible—served as the default source for correct Hebrew.

However, the fact that Ḥayyūj calls his readers to imitate لا سيما لغة الوحي وكلام النبوة 'especially the language of inspiration and prophetic speech' seems to indicate that *al-ʿibrāniyyūn* 'the Hebrews' could refer to speakers of non-biblical Hebrew as well, an idea made clearer in passages from other grammarians.

2.1.2. David ben Abraham al-Fāsī (10th c. CE)

David ben Abraham al-Fāsī (or Dāwūd ibn Ibrāhīm al-Fāsī; 10th c. CE), the famed Karaite lexicographer and grammarian from Fez, in writing his Biblical Hebrew lexicon entitled *Kitāb jāmiʿ al-alfāẓ*, also seems to be working from a framework that legitimises at least some forms of non-biblical Hebrew. Note, for example, how a particular arrangement of root letters unattested in the

[19] Khan (2013, 45; 2020, I:91–92, 107–08, 123–24) makes the point that while the Hebrew grammarians occasionally refer to other reading traditions, the Tiberian vocalisation tradition generally served as the basis for grammatical works.

Bible is still considered permissible in Hebrew (Skoss 1936–1945, I:3):

> אמא מן ד̇לך ליס במוג̇וד פי אלקראן והו ג̇איז פי אלעבראני[20]
>
> And with respect to such [a sequence of letters], it is not attested in the Bible, though it is permissible in Hebrew.

Al-Fāsī's statement clearly indicates that non-biblical forms of Hebrew did have a place in the work of the medieval grammarians. Nevertheless, even if the Bible was not the only standard of 'exemplary speakers', it certainly served as the primary standard against which proper and improper Hebrew would be determined.

2.1.3. Saadia Gaon (882–942 CE)

We may get a sense of which non-biblical texts were regarded as legitimate sources for correct Hebrew from a passage found in the Arabic introduction to Saadia Gaon's book on Hebrew poetry, *Sefer Ha-Egron*, the Arabic title of which is *Kitāb al-šiʿr al-ʿibrānī* 'The Book of Hebrew Poetry.' In describing the contents of the book, Saadia writes the following (Harkavy 1891, 50–51):

> ויתבע הד̇ה אלג׳ אלעיון פצול אכ̇ר כת̇ירה̈ יחתאג̇ אליהא אלשערא ת̇ם
> מא ראית אן אסתשהד עליה מן קול אלשערא אלאולין יוסי בן יוסי וינאי
> ואלעזר ויהושע ופינחס פעלת ד̇לך: ואמא מן קול אלשערא אלאקרבין
> אלינא פלא תג̇דני אד̇כר שיא אלא לאחמד מן כאן קולה מרצ̇יא. פאקול

[20] ≈ .أما من ذلك ليس بموجود في القرآن وهو جائز في العبراني

ולקד אגֹאד פלאן פי מא קאל ואדע עכסה אן אקול ולקד אסי פלאן פי מא קאל[21]

> And after these three principles will be many other chapters that poets need. Then, what I found I could quote from the sayings of the ancient poets, Yose ben Yose, Yannai, Eleazar, Yehoshua, and Phinehas, I did. And regarding the sayings of the poets that are closer to us [in time], you will not find me referencing anything except to praise one whose saying is pleasing (*man kāna qawluhu murḍiyyan*). Then I will say, 'So-and-so did well (*ajāda fulān*) in what he said'. And I will leave off saying the opposite, 'So-and-so did poorly (*asā fulān*) in what he said'.

This passage teaches us several things about what constitutes the corpus of correct Hebrew. It is noteworthy that, in a book of Hebrew poetry, it is not just biblical examples that are held up for imitation. Saadia also regards the sayings of non-biblical poets as worthy of emulation. Nevertheless, he makes a distinction between the 'ancient' poets and those who are closer to being contemporaries. It is only the ancient poets who are worthy of imitation without hesitation. In the case of the non-ancient poets, their saying may be מרצֿי (≈ مرضي) 'pleasing' or not. Fortunately for the reader, this task of evaluating who אגֹאד... פי מא קאל (≈ أجاد... في ما قال) 'did well in what he said' and who אסי... פי מא קאל (≈ أسى... في ما قال) 'did poorly in what he said' has already

21 ≈ ويتبع هذه ال-٣ العيون فصول آخر كثيرة يحتاج إليها الشعراء ثم ما رأيت أن أستشهد عليه من قول الشعراء الأولين يوسي بن يوسي ويَنّي وألعازار ويهوشوع وفينحاس فعلت ذلك. وأما من قول الشعراء الأقربين إلينا فلا تجدني أذكر شيئا إلا لأحمد من كان قوله مرضيا. فأقول ولقد أجاد فلان في ما قال وأدع عكسه أن أقول ولقد أسى فلان في ما قال.

been taken care of by Saadia, so that he only includes those praiseworthy poetic sayings of non-ancient poets.

The question of what exactly made these non-biblical 'ancient' poets exemplary speakers of good Hebrew is not a simple one. While the extent of our knowledge about the five poets mentioned (Yose ben Yose, Yannai, Eleazar, Yehoshua, Phinehas) is limited, they are all—with perhaps the exception of Yehoshua, about whom little is known—early *piyyuṭ* poets, known as *payṭanim* (Rabin et al. 2022).

Piyyuṭ refers to a genre of Hebrew poetry used for liturgy which developed in late antique Palestine during the Byzantine period (from the 4th/5th c. CE). The term itself (i.e., *piyyuṭ*) is derived from the Greek term for poet, ποιητής. Although it developed in Palestine, from its onset it was not developed in a context where Hebrew was the poet's mother tongue. While not departing greatly from the Hebrew of the Bible or the Mishnah, *piyyuṭ* poetry has its own distinct style. Many of its apparent morphological distinctives involve the expansion and extension of rare or unusual forms already attested in the Bible. Nevertheless, though well-grounded in the Hebrew of the Bible and the Mishnah, *piyyuṭ* is known for inventing new words and making multitudinous obscure allusions (Rand 2013; Rabin et al. 2022).

Four out of the five poets specifically mentioned by Saadia—Phinehas the Priest, Yose ben Yose, Yannai, and Eleazar ben Qalir—have the reputation of being the most outstanding of the *payṭanim*. Chronologically, Phinehas and Yose ben Yose are the earliest of these poets, having likely lived in the fourth or fifth century CE. Yannai and Eleazar ben Qalir are later, with the former spanning the late fifth and early sixth centuries and the latter the late sixth and early seventh centuries. While the *piyyuṭim* initially developed in Palestine during the Byzantine period, by the time of Saadia they had spread and flourished in the Diaspora as well (Rand 2013; Rabin et al. 2022).

Returning to Saadia's comments regarding poetry that was מרצ̇י (≈ مرضي) 'pleasing' or not, we may ask the following question: If *piyyuṭ* poetry did not develop within the context of native speakers and continue in an unbroken chain to Saadia's time, on the basis of what criteria did Saadia evaluate the *piyyuṭ* poetry? Indeed, even the style of *piyyuṭ* changed significantly over time, being divided into three phases: pre-classical, classical, and post-classical (Fleischer 2007, 1–329; Rand 2013).

Such a question highlights the real significance of Saadia's role as an evaluator of what constituted correct Hebrew. He regarded himself as responsible for providing his readers with examples of Hebrew only if they were worth emulating. By engaging in the task of *evaluating* what merits inclusion, Saadia is also *determining* the standards by which such evaluation should be carried out. Therefore, what seems to be a passive evaluation of what is correct Hebrew may actually be an implicit active formation and creation of the standards by which correct Hebrew would be judged. In this way, Saadia becomes a key figure in the process of *enregisterment* of the standard canonical form of Hebrew in the society. For his readers, he pre-selects which linguistic signs should be associated with the social types embodied in the exemplary speakers, whether figures from the biblical period or the *payṭanim*.

2.2. Comparison with the Arabic Tradition

The idea of a corpus of correct language being comprised of a sacred text—the Bible in the case of Saadia—as well as 'ancient' poetry is echoed in the Arabic grammatical tradition. Although not all of the grammarians relate to their corpus of linguistic material in precisely the same way, the *Qurʾān* and pre-Islamic poetry feature most prominently as exemplars of the standard language in the writings of the grammarians throughout the ʿAbbasid period. Of particular note here is the relation between the phrase *kalām al-ʿarab* 'the speech(?) of the Arabs' and the corpus of standard language material.

For some modern scholars, the phrase *kalām al-ʿarab* refers not to everyday colloquial speech, but to the corpus of an elevated performance register of Arabic (e.g., Brustad 2016, 148–51). Others argue that it was based on certain linguistic features such as *iʿrāb*, which, though perhaps most prominent in and characteristic of an elevated register, might also be found elsewhere. Moreover, the term *ʿarab* in this phrase does not necessarily refer to ethnic Arabs generally,[22] but to a certain linguistically defined community, whether those who were engaged in the performative culture of *kalām* (e.g., Brustad 2016, 148–51) or merely the early linguistic community of a pure Arabic speech idiom (e.g.,

---

[22] Note that the ethnic connotation of *ʿarab* itself might be a later development that occurred after the period of the early grammarians like al-Khalīl and Sībawayh (Webb 2016, 177–239).

Webb 2016, 178–80). At least among the later grammarians, however, *kalām al-ʿarab* is regarded as “the property of ancient Arabs and the ‘gold standard’ of correct Arabic (*al-fuṣḥā*)” (Webb 2016, 306). We will return to these debates later—particularly in our discussion of Sībawayh—but what is important for now is to acknowledge that the sources most characteristically cited in the grammarians as exemplars of the standard language they were documenting, namely *kalām al-ʿarab*, are the *Qurʾān* and pre-Islamic (or ‘ancient’) poetry.

2.2.1. Sībawayh (d. ca 796 CE)

The strong association of the *kalām al-ʿarab* corpus with the *Qurʾān* and pre-Islamic poetry is perhaps most evident in the role that these two sources play as prooftexts in the work of the early Arabic grammarians like Sībawayh (d. ca 796 CE). When seeking support for a particular grammatical rule or description, Sībawayh most typically draws on the *Qurʾān* and poetry (Brustad 2016, 147). From a statistical perspective, the *šawāhid* ‘proofs’ for grammatical arguments in Sībawayh’s *al-Kitāb* are comprised of roughly 1050 lines of poetry, 447 verses from the *Qurʾān*, 350 ‘speech patterns’ or idioms, and 41 proverbs (Haroun 1988, indices; Baalbaki 2008, 37).

Note, for example, how Sībawayh quotes a line from the poetry of the seventh-century Jāhiliyyah poet al-Aʿšā (d. 625 CE) in a discussion regarding adjectives (3.237–238; Haroun 1988):

وكذلك جَنوبٌ وشَمالٌ، وحَرورٌ وسَمومٌ، وقَبُولٌ ودَبُورٌ، إذا سمّيت رجلاً بشىء
منها صرفته لأنَّها صفاتٌ فى أكثر كلام العرب: سمعناهم يقولون: هذه ريحٌ
حَرورٌ، وهذه ريحٌ شَمَالٌ، وهذه الريحُ الجَنوبُ، وهذه ريحُ سَمومٌ، وهذه ريحٌ

> جَنوبٌ. سمعنا ذلك من فصحاء العرب، لا يعرفون غيره. قال الأعشى: لها
> زَجَلٌ كحَفيفِ الحَصا   دِ صادَفَ باللَّيل رِيحاً دَبورَا[23]
>
> And thus also ‘south(ern) (*janūb-un*)’, ‘north(ern) (*šamāl-un*)’, ‘hot (*ḥarūr-un*)’, ‘hot (*samūm-un*)’, ‘east(ern) (*qabūl-un*)’, and ‘west(ern) (*dabūr-un*)’. If you designate ‘a man (*rajul-an*)’ with one of these words, you would inflect it, because these are adjectives in most of *kalām al-ʿarab*. We have heard them saying, ‘this is a hot wind (*hāḏihi rīḥ-u ḥarūr-un*)’, ‘this is a northern wind (*hāḏihi rīḥ-un šamāl-un*)’, ‘this is the southern wind (*hāḏihi al-rīḥ-u al-janūb-u*)’, ‘this is a hot wind (*hāḏihi rīḥ-u samūm-un*)’, and ‘this is a southern wind (*hāḏihi rīḥ-un janūb-un*)’. We have heard such from the most eloquent of the Arabs (*fuṣaḥā al-ʿarab*), who do not know it any other way. Al-Aʿšā has said: “They [make] a sound like the rustling of the wheat stalks, which in the night met a western wind (*rīḥ-an dabūr-ā*).”

There are three key points in this passage that drive home the association of *kalām al-ʿarab* with an authoritative corpus of a particular type of language found in sources such as pre-Islamic poetry. First, the justification Sībawayh provides for his assertion that these words are to be inflected as adjectives is that they are adjectives في أكثر كلام العرب ‘in most of *kalām al-ʿarab*’. This indicates that the usage of certain words in *kalām al-ʿarab* was at least to some degree quantifiable. At the same time, however, the phrase في أكثر ‘in most of’ admits diversity within the corpus.[24] Second, the short example phrases and expressions cited by

[23] Note that the use of *tanwīn* in these examples is inconsistent in the edition of Haroun (1988).

[24] For diversity within the *ʿarabiyya*, see van Putten (2022, §2.2).

Sībawayh are said to have been heard من فصحاء العرب 'from the most eloquent of the Arabs'. Such an expression restricts the corpus to a far more limited pool than general speech. Third, and finally, the explicit citation of something that might be considered *kalām al-ʿarab* here is that of a Jāhiliyyah poet, namely al-Aʿšā (d. 625 CE).

All of this supports the claim that the phrase *kalām al-ʿarab* refers not to the everyday speech of ethnic 'Arabs', but to a specific corpus of a particular type of Arabic, and that characterised by—or at least consistent with—the sort of language found in pre-Islamic poetry. The idea that this might apply specifically to a performance register may be supported by the fact that the inflection of these words as adjectives can often be an oral component, which exists beyond the mere textual tradition and is determined by the use of *iʿrāb*. Then again, we might also imagine such an oral dimension applying to speech patterns of فصحاء العرب 'the most eloquent of the Arabs'.

A similar example is found when Sībawayh is discussing the omission of the negative particle *lā* in the case of negative oaths. After noting that the possibility of omitting *lā* is attested in *kalām al-ʿarab*, he proceeds to exemplify this by quoting a line of (presumably pre-Islamic) poetry (3.105; Haroun 1988):

> وإذا حلفتَ على فعلٍ منفيٍّ لم تغيِّره عن حاله التى كان عليها قبل أن تَحلف، وذلك قولك: واللهِ لا أَفعلُ. وقد يجوز لك — وهو من كلام العرب — أن تحذف لا وأنت تريد معناها، وذلك قولك: واللهِ أفعلُ ذاك أبداً، تريد: والله لا أَفعلُ ذلك أبداً. وقال: فحالِفْ فلا واللهِ تَهْبِطُ تَلْعةً من الأَرضِ إلا أنتَ للذل عارِفُ

> And if you swear an oath with a negated verb (i.e., not to do a thing), you do not need to alter [the verb] from the state it would be in if you did not swear an oath, like when you say [for example]: 'By God I will not do it'. And it would be permissible for you [in such cases]—seeing it is found in *kalām al-ʿarab*—to omit '*lā*' even when you still intend [a negated] meaning, like when you say [for example]: 'By God I will (not) do it ever (*abad-an*)'. And [as the poet] has said, "So make an alliance, but by God you will (not) go down into a valley from the earth without being acquainted with lowliness."

Once again, such a passage demonstrates the close association between grammatical rules, *kalām al-ʿarab*, and poetry. It was not only pre-Islamic poetry, however, that provided the exemplary linguistic material of *kalām al-ʿarab*. As noted above, passages from the *Qurʾān* can be marshalled as exemplary linguistic material in a similar way. Note that Sībawayh may support his grammatical prescriptions by noting that the same type of feature is كثير في القرآن 'frequent in the *Qurʾān*' (e.g., 2.39, 3.143) or stating that مثل هذا في القرآن كثير 'the like occurs in the *Qurʾān* frequently' (3.162).

The fact that Sībawayh could draw on linguistic examples from the *Qurʾān* or pre-Islamic poetry (among other sources) underscores the importance of his role as an evaluator of linguistic material. Because internal linguistic diversity is attested in the *kalām al-ʿarab* corpus, it was ultimately up to Sībawayh to determine which examples would be valuable and worthy of emulation for his audience. Indeed, even though it may seem as if Sībawayh is merely relaying data and examples from pre-Islamic poetry, the *Qur'ān*, and other sources, he regularly makes his own evaluative judgments.

In many cases, Sībawayh describes a certain morphological or syntactic feature as عربي جيد 'good Arabic' (Haroun 1988):

> والتنوينُ عربيٌّ جيّدٌ
>
> And *tanwīn* is good Arabic. (1.194)
>
> وإن قدّمتَ الاسمَ فهو عربيٌّ جيّد، كما كان ذلك عربيًا جيّدا، وذلك قولك: زيداً ضربتُ
>
> And if you make the noun come first, this is good Arabic, just like it is good Arabic when you say [for example], 'I hit Zayd (*zayd-an ḍarabtu*)'. (1.80)
>
> إلاّ أنك إن شئت نصبتَه كما تنصب زيداً ضربتُه، فهو عربيٌّ جَيّدٌ
>
> But if you want to make it accusative, just like you make it so in the phrase 'Zayd, I hit him (*zayd-an ḍarabtuhu*)', this is good Arabic. (1.104)

Nevertheless, such cases of عربي جيد 'good Arabic' may be accompanied by quotations from the *Qur'ān* and pre-Islamic poetry to further buttress the claim (e.g., 1.56).

What is perhaps of more interest for our comparison are those cases where Sībawayh appears to cite a contemporary as an exemplary speaker of Arabic. In these cases, he might describe his source as من يوثق بعربيته 'one whose *'arabiyya* can be trusted' (Haroun 1988):

وحدّثنى أبو الخطّاب أنه سمع من يوثق بعربيته من العرب يُنشِد هذا البيت

> And Abū al-Ḫaṭṭāb told me that he had heard an Arab, whose *ʿarabiyya* can be trusted (*man yūṯaqu bi-ʿarabiyyatihi*), reciting this line of poetry… (2.111)

سمعت من يوثَق بعربيته من العرب يقول: هذهْ أَمَةُ الله. فيُسكِّن

> I heard one of the Arabs whose *ʿarabiyya* can be trusted (*man yūṯaqu bi-ʿarabiyyatihi*) saying, 'This (*hāḏih[i]*) is the handmaiden of God', and he did not pronounce a vowel after [the final *hāʾ* in the word *hāḏihi*]. (4.198)

In other cases, the *ʿarabiyya* of his source is not just described as 'good' or 'trustworthy' but rather as 'pleasing' (Haroun 1988):

ومنْهم من يفتح إذا التقى ساكنان على كل حال، إلا فى الألف واللام والألف الْخفيفة. فزعم الخليل أنهم شبهوه بأَيْنَ وكَيْفَ وسَوْفَ وأشباهِ ذلك، وفعلوا به إذ جاءوا بالألف واللام والألف الخفيفة ما فَعَلَ الأوّلون، وهم بنو أَسَدٍ وغيرُهم من بنى تميم. وسمعناه ممن تُرْضى عربيته

> And there are those among them who pronounce *fatḥa* if two consonants without a vowel meet in any circumstance, except with *alif-lām* and light *alif*. Al-Ḫalīl claims that they compare it to the words 'where?' (*ayna*), 'how?' (*kayfa*), 'will' (*sawfa*), and the like. And when it occurs with *alif-lām* or light *alif*, they do with it what those of former times did, namely Banū Asad, and others from Banū Tamīm. We heard this from someone whose *ʿarabiyya* is pleasing (*mimman turḍā ʿarabiyyatuhu*). (3.533)

وذلك قولك: هذا الضاربُ زيداً، فصار فى معنى [هذا] الّذى ضرَبَ زيداً، وعَمِلَ عَمَله، لأنّ الألفَ واللام مَنَعَتا الإضافة وصارتا بمنزلة التنوين. وكذلك: هذا الضاربُ الرّجلَ، وهو وجهُ الكلام. وقد قال قومٌ من العرب تُرْضَى عربيَّتُهم: هذا الضاربُ الرجلِ

> And this is like you saying [for example]: 'This is the hitter (of) Zayd (acc.)', the meaning of which is really more like 'this is the one who hit Zayd'. He performed his action, since the *alif-lām* (i.e., the definite article) prevented an *iḍāfa* construction and came to have the same grammatical status as *tanwīn*. And this is like the phrase, 'This is the hitter (of) the man (acc.)', and this is the typical way of *kalām*. And a group of Arabs whose *ʿarabiyya* is pleasing (*qawm min al-ʿarab turḍā ʿarabiyyatuhum*) have said: 'This is the hitter of the man (gen.)'. (1.181–182)

It is not entirely clear why the Arabic of these contemporaries of Sībawayh was regarded as trustworthy or pleasing. Perhaps it was because they were regarded as reliable tradents or reciters of the *kalām al-ʿarab* corpus (Brustad 2016, 153). After all, note that proper language use is described in the first passage here as being consistent with ما فعل الأولون 'what the ancients/those of former times did'. On the other hand, perhaps their own native dialects of Arabic exhibited certain linguistic features, such as *iʿrāb* and verbal mood, which endeared them to Sībawayh's linguistic aesthetic judgment. Maybe there was some degree of overlap between these two possibilities. In any case, Sībawayh's role in selecting such sources is significant.

While on the surface it may seem as if Sībawayh is merely transmitting linguistic data from sources that are considered reliable by consensus, there is much more going on by way of facilitating enregisterment and standardisation. By making decisions regarding what belongs in the corpus, Sībawayh is helping pre-determine which linguistic signs might come to be associated with the idealised 'speaker' of the *Qur'ān*, the exemplary speakers (or reciters) of pre-Islamic poetry, those contemporaries with trustworthy Arabic, etc. After all, as van Putten (2022, 47–98) has shown, there was considerable variation in *al-ʿarabiyya*, so that there was not a simple monolithic entity that the grammarians could document objectively. By determining and selecting what forms of *al-ʿarabiyya* are 'good', 'trustworthy', or 'pleasing', Sībawayh is participating in constructing the *ʿarabiyya* itself. Rather than being merely a neutral observer, he is helping to shape the very perceptions of his audience regarding who constitutes an exemplary speaker of the *ʿarabiyya* worthy of emulation.

When commenting on these phrases, Brustad (2016, 152) insightfully notes that Sībawayh both "admits that [elevated] authority [of his sources] and already begins to undermine it: although he is reporting the judgment of experts, he is the one determining who those experts are." On the other hand, Webb (2016, 305) argues that referencing one 'whose Arabic is pleasing' is actually indicative of the fact that "power remains with Sībawayh's readership to appraise the language." For Webb, in part due to the prevalence of second-person verbal forms (e.g., 'you say...') in the *Kitāb*, Sībawayh regards his readership as the primary creators of the language. Many of his grammatical discussions thus use his readers' speech habits as a starting point. Nevertheless, even if this is the case, we may note that it is still Sībawayh who is deciding what to include and thereby constructing how they understand their own language. In any case, in this way, Sībawayh and his *Kitāb* would play a central role in the process of standardisation and institutionalisation (see chapter 3, §2.1.7) of the *ʿarabiyya* over the course of the following century.

At this point, we must return to the nuances of the phrase *kalām al-ʿarab* in Sībawayh, given its close association with the 'corpus', data pool, or object of study in his *Kitāb*.[25] While Sībawayh is clearly interested in 'the speech of the Arabs' (Baalbaki 2008, 18–20), the fact that his informants are qualified as those who have trustworthy Arabic has led scholars to propose more restricted definitions of the phrase *kalām al-ʿarab* than merely denoting Arabic speech generally.

For Brustad (2016, 148–51), for example, the term *kalām* in the phrase *kalām al-ʿarab* refers to the corpus of a certain elevated performance register of Arabic, primarily comprised of the *Qurʾān* and pre-Islamic poetry. The term *al-ʿarab* in the same phrase thus refers not to ethnic Arabs more generally but to those who were engaged in the performative culture of *kalām*. She finds support for this claim in how Ibn Qutayba (d. 889 CE) lays out categories related to language in his work *al-Maʿārif*.[26] As she points out (2016, 145), his categories are all concerned with how the 'language and lore' of pre-Islamic (and early Islamic) Arabia were studied and transmitted. That later periods exhibit a mark-

---

[25] Note, however, that the phrase does not actually occur that frequently in the *Kitāb* (Webb 2016, 303–04).

[26] For topics involving language, he groups أصحاب القراءات 'Qurʾān Reading Authorities', قرّاء الألحان 'Readers who Perform with Melodies', النسابون وأصحاب الأخبار 'Genealogists and Oral Historians', and رواة الشعر وأصحاب الغريب والنحو 'Poetry Reciters, Lexicographers, and Grammarians' (Brustad 2016, 145).

edly different categorisation highlights the fact that early 'grammatical' work, such as that of Sībawayh, developed in close connection with the *Qur'ān* and pre-Islamic poetry. At an early period, the term *naḥwiyyūn*—used later to mean 'grammarians'—might have referred only to those concerned with how the *Qur'ān* and poetry were recited or performed. Indeed, for Brustad and others, the work of the early Arabic 'grammarians' was not concerned so much with spoken Arabic as with performed Arabic (Talmon 2003, 35–37; Carter 2004, 5; Brustad 2016, 146).[27] And yet, despite her emphasis on a performance register, Brustad still acknowledges Sībawayh's esteem for the Ḥijāzī dialect, highlighting his statement that والحجازية هي اللغة الأولى القدمى 'Ḥijāzī is the first and oldest language variety' (3.278; Haroun 1988). Such a statement conveys a sense of historicity, perhaps reflecting a belief that a contemporaneous performance register was once a more colloquial language (Brustad 2010).

---

[27] On this point, Brustad argues that some early grammarians did not limit their discussion of grammatical rules to a fixed consonantal text but rather included a variable array of performances. She illustrates this by citing the discussion of the consonantal sequence فى ام الكتاب (Az-Zukhruf [43.4]) in al-Farrā''s (d. 822/823 CE) ninth-century work *Ma'ānī al-qur'ān*. While the common *Qur'ānic* reading today is فِي أُمِّ الْكِتَابِ, al-Farrā' (1.5–6; Najātī and al-Najjār 1955) admits that there are two possibilities for reading this word. While some read it as أُمّ, others read it as إِمّ (Brustad 2016, 147). Note also that most of the attested data found in Sībawayh are introduced as something 'heard' rather than something merely textual (Baalbaki 2008, 35–38).

For Webb (2016), on the other hand, the precise content of the phrase *kalām al-ʿarab* in Sībawayh and subsequent grammarians is largely dependent on the continually evolving meaning of its latter component, namely *al-ʿarab*. During the period of the early grammarians like al-Khalīl and Sībawayh, it is unlikely that the term *ʿarab* had yet acquired its strong ethnic connotation, which would be much more familiar to later generations—and moderns for that matter. At the time of Sībawayh, the term *ʿarab*, at least in the works of the philologists, referred not to an ethnic group but to a speech community. Arabness was associated with a "unique, pure speech idiom derived from religious practice" (Webb 2016, 180). Though, for Webb, *kalām al-ʿarab* was not necessarily a performance register, he notes that the emphasis on one whose Arabic was trustworthy further restricts Sībawayh's data pool beyond the collective community of Arabic speakers.[28] While Webb's view might allow for contemporary colloquial speech to be admitted into the corpus of *kalām al-ʿarab*, so long as it is from a trustworthy source, he still recognises the special place that poetry holds in Sībawayh's *Kitāb* (Webb 2016, 179–80, 303–06).[29]

---

[28] Note that for Marogy (2010b, 7), it seems that 'trustworthy Arabs' were closely connected with what Sībawayh terms اللغة العربية القديمة الجيدة 'good old Arabic' (4.473; Haroun 1988) and the Ḥijāzī dialect.

[29] Compare the view of Marogy (2010b, 30, 45), who argues that "the highly esteemed speech of the Arabs relegates the *Qurʾān* and poetry to a subsidiary role" and that "the speech of the Arabs was Sībawayhi's first source of material evidence, and, as such, it was given priority above the *Qurʾān* and poetry." What is intended by such 'priority', however, seems to be that the language was the principal object of study,

Although there are differences between a view like Brustad's and that of Webb, there is also considerable overlap. After all, it is not so much a question of whether Sībawayh was documenting a performance register—in many cases he undoubtedly was—but a question of whether that was *all* he was doing or even *primarily* what he was doing. There is no doubt that the *Qur'ān* and pre-Islamic poetry (when properly recited) constitute exemplary sources for Sībawayh. Where the debate lies is whether the linguistic material of contemporary speakers of colloquial Arabic might also be regarded with favour by the Persian grammarian.[30] As noted above, perhaps the presence of *iʿrāb* and verbal mood in an Arabic speaker's dialect might have made him

---

whereas the *Qur'ān* and poetry feature to provide "mere means of attestation." While this is not inaccurate, we might highlight that treating the *Qur'ān* and ancient poetry as main sources for 'means of attestation' is quite significant. Moreover, Marogy (2010b, 7) is also careful to point out that Sībawayh's primary goal "was not the speech of Arabs in general but that of trustworthy Arabs."

[30] On one occasion in Sībawayh's *Kitāb*, he describes a piece of linguistic evidence that he heard personally from two Arab men as follows (2.27–28; Haroun 1988): ومن جوازِ الرفع فى هذا الباب أنّى سمعت رجلينِ من العرب عربيّينِ يقولان: كان عبدُ الله حَسْبُكَ به رجلا 'And with respect to the permissibility of the nominative in such a category, I heard two men from amongst the Arabs, Arabs themselves, saying, "Abdallah was a man sufficient for you"'. This sort of datum, though rare, may indicate that Sībawayh might have heard linguistic examples from the real conversations of contemporary speakers of various Arabic varieties.

one whose Arabic was trustworthy or pleasing.[31] Another question connected to this issue concerns whether the 'corpus' of *kalām al-ʿarab* was considered largely closed at the time of Sībawayh. The evidence would seem to indicate that it may not have been totally closed—or at least not static—in all its aspects and facets.

While it may not be possible to answer all these questions with certainty, we might propose that there were multiple factors that went into Sībawayh's selection process with respect to trustworthy Arabic and informed what constitued *kalām al-ʿarab* on the whole. On one hand, the types of language associated with orally-performed formal 'texts' of inherent prestige in the society seem to have been regarded as exemplary Arabic. This is certainly the case with the *Qurʾān*, given its significance for Islam. Pre-Islamic poetry, though likely enjoying some prestige in society already, was amplified in its importance after the rise of Islam, due to its chronological proximity to the *Qurʾān*.[32] On the other hand, more objective measures, like the presence of certain linguistic features such as *iʿrāb* and verbal mood, might also have

---

[31] I would like to thank Phillip Stokes for suggesting this possibility and discussing its implications with me.

[32] Webb (2016, 306) notes that "as grammarians codified the rules, certain Arabs, especially those who transmitted poetry from the past, emerged as embodying the purest form of the language presumably on account of their proximity to the period of the Qurʾan's revelation." According to Webb, however, the homogenous conceptualisation of *kalām al-ʿarab* as the "property of ancient Arabs" and the exemplar of pure Arabic *par excellence*, common in later grammarians, had not yet developed at the time of Sībawayh.

been sufficient for a linguistic source to be regarded as trustworthy. This would, of course, allow for dialectal examples to be included in Sībawayh's *Kitāb* if their speakers exhibited such linguistic features in their dialect. At the same time, it would also help explain why the *Qurʾān* and pre-Islamic poetry feature so heavily in his grammar, since these sources meet both criteria with flying colours.[33]

Nevertheless, given the fact that most Hebrew grammarians we are dealing with are from a later period, it is not so crucial to determine with precision what Sībawayh meant by *kalām al-ʿarab*. After all, as Webb (2016, 303–04) points out, he does not use the phrase as often as we might think—only eighteen times in the first two volumes. Moreover, he does not appear to be documenting just one single form of Arabic with a rigid set of rules. For Sībawayh, the language itself exists in multiple forms and multiple streams; it is diverse and somewhat flexible. Indeed, according to Webb (2016, 306), some discourses of this period "portrayed Arabs as a broad speech community of varied dialects (akin also to the Qurʾan's references to the indefinite *ʿarabī*)." What is more important for our purposes is how later Arabic

---

[33] Note, however, that at an early period various readings of the *Qurʾān* did not have a systematic application of *iʿrāb*; its distribution was more restricted than in certain descriptions of Classical Arabic. The consistent and systematic application of case vowels in recitations of the *Qurʾān* might itself be a development owing something to the work of early philologists and grammarians. For more on case in the consonantal text of the *Qurʾān* and the *qirāʾāt*, see Stokes (2017, 65–95).

grammarians would develop the concept of *kalām al-ʿarab* in the wake of Sībawayh's grammar.

For if the medieval Hebrew grammarians were drawing on or influenced by Sībawayh—a likely supposition—it is plausible that they were reading him through the lens of ninth- and tenth-century Arabic grammatical thought. As we will see, it was during this period that the term *ʿarab* shifted from signifying a speech community to indicating an ethnic community. This semantic and cultural shift would, in turn, have substantial implications for the meaning of the phrase *kalām al-ʿarab* in the work of later grammarians and philologists.

2.2.2. al-Farrāʾ (d. 822/823 CE)

The term *kalām al-ʿarab* appears to be much more frequent in al-Farrāʾ's (d. 822/823 CE) *Maʿānī al-qurʾān*. In addition to accompanying the term with citations from the *Qurʾān* (see above in §1.2.3), al-Farrāʾ often relates *kalām al-ʿarab* to poetic verse. When discussing the omission of a *wāw* or *yāʾ* at the end of a verbal form, he writes the following (2.117–118; Najātī and al-Najjār 1955):

> وقوله: ويَدْعُ الإِنْسَانُ حذفت الواو منها فى اللفظ ولم تُحذف فى المعنى؛ لأنها فى موضع رفع، فكان حذفها باستقبالها اللام السَّاكنة. ومثلها (سَنَدْعُ الزَّبَانِيَةَ) وكذلك (وَسَوْفَ يُؤْتِ اللّٰهُ المُؤْمِنِينَ)... ولو كُنَّ بالياء والواو كان صَوابًا. وهذا من كلام العرب. قال الشاعر: كفاك كَفٌّ
>
> ما تُليق درهما   جُودًا وأخرى تُعْطِ بالسيف الدَّما

And when he says, "and man invokes (*yadʿu*)" (Al-Isra [17.11]), the *wāw* is omitted from it in the word (or 'pronunciation'?), though it is not omitted in the meaning,

> since it is in the indicative mood, and its omission occurs when it precedes *lām sākina*. Similar cases include 'we will call (*sanadʿu/sanadʿū*) the angels of hell' and 'God will give (*yuʾti/yuʾtī*) the believers'... Whether such occurs with *yāʾ* or with *wāw*, both are correct (*ṣawāb*). And this is part of *kalām al-ʿarab*. [As] the poet says, "Your hands—one spares a *dirham* generously, but the other gives (*tuʿṭi/tuʿṭī*) blood with the sword."

After presenting the grammatical issue and explaining it, al-Farrāʾ then proceeds to exemplify it by turning to an example from *kalām al-ʿarab*, which in this case entails a line of poetry. Interestingly, we may recall that the line of poetry cited here is precisely the same one cited for the same grammatical phenomenon in another passage in al-Farrāʾ's *Maʿānī al-qurʾān* (see §1.2.3). This may indicate that al-Farrāʾ had at his disposal a sort of stock list of poetic examples that were associated with illustrating various and particular grammatical phenomena.

While the association between poetry and *kalām al-ʿarab* is the most relevant part of this passage for the present discussion, there are a couple other noteworthy points. First, the particular issue under discussion is an orthographic one, namely whether certain verbal forms are spelled with *wāw* or *yāʾ*. As such, it textualises *kalām al-ʿarab* to a degree.[34] Second, after explaining the issue, al-Farrāʾ asserts that such orthographies are صواب 'correct', a word he uses hundreds of times throughout *Maʿānī al-qurʾān*. This is especially conspicuous when compared with the almost

[34] On the other hand, one might consider the discussion relevant for vowel length, in which case it would also have an oral component.

complete absence of this word in Sībawayh.[35] These two points highlight that the processes of both codification and standardisation had advanced since the time of Sībawayh.

Advancement in the processes of codification and standardisation is also apparent in the following passage, in which a saying about a lizard's 'burrow' or 'hole' is related, likely due to the particular nature of the *iʿrāb* on the words involved (2.74; Najātī and al-Najjār 1955):

ومِمّا يرويه نحويُّونا الأَوَّلون أن العرب تقول: هذا جُحْرُ ضَبٍّ خَرِبٍ

> And from what our grammarians of former times (*naḥwiyyūnā al-awwalūn*) report, the Arabs (*al-ʿarab*) say, 'And this is the destroyed hole of a lizard'.

That al-Farrāʾ references نحويونا الأولون 'our grammarians of former times' demonstrates that there was already a codified tradition upon which he was drawing. Moreover, it is noteworthy that he does not cite the source of the saying—i.e., *al-ʿarab* 'the Arabs'—directly, but relies on the report of past grammarians. This speaks to a certain growing distance between the grammarian and the object of his study, especially when compared with earlier grammarians like Sībawayh.

2.2.3. Ibn Sallām al-Jumaḥī (d. 845/846 CE)

A close association between poetry and *kalām al-ʿarab* is also evidenced in *Ṭabaqāt fuḥūl al-šuʿarāʾ* by Ibn Sallām al-Jumaḥī (d. 845/846 CE), the famous grammarian and literary scholar of

[35] According to my count, it appears only once, in 4.329 (Haroun 1988).

Baṣra. In his introduction, he writes the following about his classification of poets (1.23–24; Šākir 1997):

> ففصَّلنا الشعراءَ من أهل الجاهليّةِ والإسلام، والمُخَضْرَمين الذين كَانوا فى الجاهليّةِ وأدركُوا الإسلامَ، فنزَّلناهم منازلَهم، واحتجَجْنا لكلِّ شاعرٍ بما وجَدْنا له من حُجَّة، وما قال فيه العلماء. وقد اختلف الناسُ والرواة فيهم. فنظر قوم من أهْل العِلم بالشعرِ، والنَّفاذ فى كلامِ العرب، والعلمِ بالعربيّة، إذا اختَلَفتِ الرُّواةُ فقالوا بآرائهم

> We have categorised the poets of the Jāhiliyyah, those from the time of Islam, and those who straddle both periods. We have set them in their positions and compiled the evidence we found for every poet and what scholars have said regarding them. Now the people and the narrators have expressed different [opinions] with respect to them. So a group of scholars of poetry (*šiʿr*), those possessed of comprehensive familiarity with *kalām al-ʿarab* and expertise in the *ʿarabiyya*, observed that if the narrators differed, they asserted their belief in their opinions.

The fact that Ibn Sallām groups *šiʿr* ‘poetry’, *kalām al-ʿarab*, and *al-ʿarabiyya* together in his description of a particular group of scholars is significant. It is also noteworthy that while *šiʿr* and *al-ʿarabiyya* are each described as a branch of knowledge (i.e., *ʿilm*), Ibn Sallām uses the term *nafāḏ* to describe expertise in *kalām al-ʿarab*. The word *nafāḏ*, which is rare for such a context, generally means something like ‘penetration’, ‘passing through’, ‘effectiveness’, or ‘execution’ (Lane 1863–1893). Given the context here, then, it is possible that it refers to a comprehensive familiarity based on passing through the corpus of *kalām al-ʿarab*.[36] Alternatively, it could also indicate an ability to implement the content of *kalām al-ʿarab* with all its conventions and rules. In either case, this may point to the fact that *kalām al-ʿarab* was regarded as a corpus in which one could be an expert. Finally, we should also note that, beyond the obvious association between *kalām al-ʿarab* and poetry expressed above and throughout the work, Ibn Sallām also adduces examples from the *Qurʾān* to illustrate *kalām al-ʿarab* in his book (see, e.g., 1.22).

2.2.4. Ibn al-Sarrāj (d. 928/929 CE)

Although the phrase *kalām al-ʿarab* occurs frequently in Ibn al-Sarrāj's (d. 928/929 CE) *Kitāb al-uṣūl fī al-naḥw*, his very first use of it is telling. When explaining the purpose of *naḥw* 'grammar' in the first line of his introduction (1.35; Fatlī 1996), he specifically holds up *kalām al-ʿarab* as the object of study (Wahba 2023):

> النحو إنما أريد به أن ينحو المتكلم إذا تعلمه كلام العرب، وهو علم استخرجه المتقدمون فيه من استقراء كلام العرب، حتى وقفوا منه على الغرض الذي قصده المبتدئون بهذه اللغة، فباستقراء كلام العرب فاعلم: أن الفاعل رفع، والمفعول به نصب...
>
> All I mean by the term 'grammar (*naḥw*)' is that the (beginner) speaker, if he studies it, would aim at *kalām al-ʿarab*. And it (i.e., grammar) is a branch of knowledge that those who were first in the field derived by investigating

[36] Though from a later date, note for the sake of comparison that Ibn Bashkuwal (d. 1183 CE) uses the phrase أهل النفاذ في الحديث '*Ahl al-nafāḏ* in hadith' (*Kitāb al-ṣila fī tārīḫ aʾimmat al-andalus*, 217; Maʿrūf 1955).

> *kalām al-ʿarab*, so that from it they could arrive at [an understanding of] the purpose for which beginners [learn] this language. And with respect to the investigation of *kalām al-ʿarab*, know that the subject is nominative, the object is accusative...

For Ibn al-Sarrāj, then, the origin of the field of grammar itself was based on an investigation of *kalām al-ʿarab* by the early grammarians. Although we have translated the key term here استقراء as 'investigating', Webb (2016, 309–10) suggests that it should be rendered as 'close reading'. This would imply that Ibn al-Sarrāj was actually conceiving of the corpus of *kalām al-ʿarab* as something one could access in written form. This would be consistent with the fact that, elsewhere in his book, he not only adduces examples from the *Qurʾān* and poetry to exemplify *kalām al-ʿarab* (see, e.g., 2.95), but quotes the earlier grammarians' descriptions of it as well (see, e.g., 1.260). On either reading, however, we find reflected here a conception of *kalām al-ʿarab* that is far more static and far less fluid than that of the early grammarians.

Indeed, while Sībawayh might have allowed for an untidy presentation of the linguistic diversity of Arabic, Ibn al-Sarrāj's grammar has a more pedagogical bent, in which grammar is presented as a series of rules that the beginning learner must acquire in order to imitate *kalām al-ʿarab* (Webb 2016, 309–11; Wahba 2023). While Sībawayh might have been more concerned with how a speaker's intent mapped onto grammatical form, Ibn al-Sarrāj encourages his readers to imitate the grammatical rules consistent with what is attested in *kalām al-ʿarab*. By requiring the derivation of clear and consistent rules from *kalām al-ʿarab*, however, Ibn al-Sarrāj precludes any possibility of continued development or evolution in the language. At this point, then, *kalām al-ʿarab* is no longer a living organism but merely a relic from the past (Webb 2016, 309–11). Indeed, Marogy (2010b, 35–36) argues that, already by the time of al-Mubarrad (d. 898 CE), "first hand enquiries about the speech of the Arabs were a practical impossibility, for 'good old Arabic' had ceased to be a living language by then."

Part of the reason for this change is the continued evolution and development, semantically and culturally, of the term *ʿarab*. While the term *ʿarab* might have been more prone to refer to a speech community at the time of Sībawayh and al-Khalīl, it had taken on stronger ethnic connotations over the course of the ninth century. By the time of Ibn al-Sarrāj, the term *ʿarab*, along with its historical referents, was being reimagined and recontextualised so as to bring it more into conformity with the various cultural connotations of the term *aʿrāb* 'Bedouin'. As a result, *kalām al-ʿarab* was no longer the language of a particular living speech community, but the idealised speech of the desert Bedouin from the 'ancient' past, who had now become the lone preserve of proper and pure Arabic (Webb 2016, 311).[37]

Ibn al-Sarrāj's grammar is thus a key work in the process of standardisation. After all, it is widely regarded as "one of the first codifications of Arabic grammar in terms of 'correct principles'

---

[37] The fact that these desert-dwelling speakers of proper Arabic were distant geographically and chronologically is an important development that has relevance for another aspect of language ideology to which we will return in the following section (see §3.0).

(*uṣūl*) backed by a rational framework (*ʿilal*)" (Webb 2016, 311). Suleiman (2011, 3) might call it a significant part of the "grammar-making" aspect of "corpus-planning." From this point on, if not already before, to study *kalām al-ʿarab* was to concern oneself with the purest, most correct form of Arabic from the distant past, belonging to "ancient Arabs" (Webb 2016, 306) and attested in sources like the *Qurʾān*, pre-Islamic poetry, and indirectly through earlier grammarians like Sībawayh.[38]

Given the wider purposes of our book, it is worth noting that the conception of the standard language corpus in later Arabic grammarians like Ibn al-Sarrāj is probably much more relevant for our comparison with the Hebrew grammarians than that of Sībawayh. After all, most of the Hebrew grammarians examined in this book were contemporaries with or lived within a century or so after Ibn al-Sarrāj. Even though they were almost certainly familiar with Sībawayh's *Kitāb* and read it, it is probable that they read it with perspectives on *kalām al-ʿarab* and *al-ʿarab* closer to those of the later Arabic grammarians. As we will see in the rest of the book, that the Hebrew grammarians exhibit greatest similarity with the ideology of the ninth- and tenth-century

[38] Marogy (2010b, 45) argues that the prescriptive turn in the nature of later grammarians' work is due to the fact that they no longer had access to "real data," but—aside from the *Qurʾān* and poetry—were totally dependent on Sībawayh for the corpus of real spoken Arabic. Webb (2016, 315) similarly argues that, among the later grammarians, "the rules taught... by the philologists appear faithful reproductions of the 'real' *kalām al-ʿarab*."

grammarians—rather than earlier grammarians like Sībawayh—is a recurring theme throughout our analysis.

2.3. Analysis

The end of the preceding section (§1.0) highlighted the tension between Hebrew and Arabic being treated as cultural possessions of native speakers, on the one hand, and the expectation that, within a standard language ideology, the canonical form of the language should exist outside the members of the society, on the other. The analysis of the present section has provided further clarity to resolve that tension. The Hebrews and the Arabs of the phrases *lughat al-ʿibrāniyyīn* 'the language of the Hebrews' and *kalām al-ʿarab* 'the speech of the Arabs'—at least in the writings of the later Arabic grammarians—are not the grammarians' contemporaries. Rather, they are the 'exemplary speakers' (see chapter 3, §2.2) of the 'ancient' past. Indeed, a prominent trend of similarity between the Hebrew and Arabic grammatical traditions on this point concerns the temporal location of the exemplary speakers of the standard language and their 'corpus'.

In each tradition, the 'exemplary speakers' worthy of imitation are those associated with an ancient sacred text, namely the Bible in the case of the Hebrew tradition and the *Qurʾān* in the case of the Arabic tradition. Indeed, the *Qurʾān* may be conceived of as the production of an abstract ideal 'speaker'. And yet, these sacred texts did not comprise the corpus of exemplary language by themselves. In the Hebrew tradition, the language of the Bible was supplemented by both Rabbinic Hebrew and the

Byzantine tradition of Hebrew poetry known as *piyyuṭ*. In the Arabic tradition, the language of the *Qurʾān* was supplemented primarily by pre-Islamic poetry, though other sources were sometimes admitted as well. Such a closed corpus of historical pure language is probably what is meant by the phrase *kalām al-ʿarab* in much of the Arabic grammatical tradition contemporaneous with the Hebrew grammarians examined in our book, even if earlier grammarians like Sībawayh might have interacted with at least some contemporary 'spoken' examples.

This aspect of the grammarians' language ideology helps resolve the tension highlighted earlier. Because the present communities viewed themselves as connected to their ancestors, the canonical language can still be regarded as a cultural possession. Nevertheless, because proficiency in the standard language is found in those 'exemplary speakers' of the past, the canonical form of the language does still exist outside of the typical language user contemporary with the grammarians.

There are two further important points to be made about these 'ancient' corpora of exemplary speakers. First, in both the Hebrew and Arabic traditions, these ancient corpora admit a variety of sources leading to internal linguistic diversity. Biblical Hebrew, Rabbinic Hebrew, and the Hebrew of the *piyyuṭim* differ considerably. While *Qurʾānic* Arabic and the Arabic of pre-Islamic poetry may be considered more similar, there are still significant differences. Sībawayh himself acknowledges linguistic diversity among his sources, sometimes with conflicting grammatical realisations both being considered عربي جيد 'good Arabic'.

The second point to be made here concerns the role of the grammarian as an evaluator of language and participant in the process of constructing the standard language. While the existence of a somewhat fixed ancient corpus might seem to necessitate that the grammarian be no more than an objective anthologist, grammarians of both traditions were far more determinative of the grammar itself than one might imagine. When Saadia says that he may reference a more recent poet מן כאן קולה מרצ̇יא (≈ من كان قوله مرضيا) 'whose saying was pleasing' or Sībawayh relays that he heard a grammatical feature in the language of one من ترضى عربيته 'whose *ʿarabiyya* is pleasing', they are implicitly conveying to their audience that they too should regard such speakers and language as aesthetically exemplary. By making such judgments, these medieval grammarians were not merely reporting the grammar but institutionalising what they regarded as good grammar. By means of this process, we might also suggest that the grammarians were (at least implicitly) determining the set of linguistic signs that could then be enregistered by their readers to the social targets associated with the exemplary speakers.

Despite the similar phraseology found in Saadia and Sībawayh, however, the chronological gap between the two likely entails a difference in the nature of this process. At the earliest stages of the Arabic tradition, as in Sībawayh, the grammarian is simply making decisions as to what may be considered as belonging to the *ʿarabiyya*. In making sense of a vast array of linguistic material, Sībawayh had to make decisions about organisation, inclusion, and exclusion. This does not necessarily entail prescription, since Sībawayh himself often admits internal diversity within the *ʿarabiyya*. Among the later Arabic grammarians, however, perhaps when standard language ideology was on the rise, grammatical works take on a more prescriptive nature and grammatical rules become more static, as in the case of Ibn al-Sarrāj. Because this was the period during which Saadia worked, it is plausible that even his understanding of Sībawayh was filtered through the later grammarians' accelerated evolution of the standard language ideology. Rather than describe the grammar, these later grammarians prescribe the grammar. Instead of merely documenting the language, they institutionalise their preferred forms thereof, even if drawing largely on the work of earlier grammarians. Moreover, by locating the corpus of standard language in the past—against which corpus they judge more contemporary expressions—they also confer a degree of legitimacy on their own judgments by means of historicisation (see chapter 3, §2.1.8).

And yet, because the Hebrew grammatical tradition was not nearly as developed as the Arabic tradition at the time of Saadia, there are also aspects of Saadia's pioneering role in the history of Hebrew grammar that are more reminiscent of Sībawayh than of Ibn al-Sarrāj. All of this might explain why Saadia appears to reflect a conception of a standard language corpus much more in line with that of the later Arabic grammarians, but at the same time exhibits some of the same phraseology and ideology as Sībawayh in terms of his role as a language evaluator.

3.0. The 'Fieldwork' *Topos*: أستمع كلام السوقة

Although the preceding section demonstrates that the 'exemplary speakers' of Hebrew and Arabic were located in the 'ancient' past for the medieval grammarians, there are hints that they might occasionally admit data from one closer to their time or even from a contemporary. After all, Saadia may cite a poet of more recent times who אג׳אד... פי מא קאל (≈ أجاد... في ما قال) 'did well in what he said' (§2.1.3). For Ḥayyūj, there seems to be an identity between the Tiberian vocalisation and the linguistic practice and speech patterns of *al-ʿibrāniyyūn* 'the Hebrews' (§1.1.2). Sībawayh, similarly, references data from one من يوثق بعربيته 'whose *ʿarabiyya* can be trusted' (§2.2.1). Presumably, this was someone who knew the corpus and was a reliable judge of acceptable or proper linguistic form, perhaps a poet steeped in the poetic tradition, a collector of poetry, or a lexicographer of rare words. It remains possible, however, that there were also those whose spoken language, perhaps due to the presence of *iʿrāb* and verbal mood, was regarded as a reliable example of trustworthy Arabic. In any case, all of this suggests that there were at least some contemporaries to whom the grammarians could go for reliable data.

What we will see, however, is that, at least at a certain point in each tradition, this group of contemporary 'exemplary speakers' comes to be found 'out in the wild' or 'off the beaten path' as it were. In the Hebrew tradition, the reliable informants are found in the city of Tiberias on the Sea of Galilee, whereas the reliable informants in the Arabic tradition are the Bedouin of the desert. In either case, at least as an ideological construct, the grammarians have to venture out and conduct 'fieldwork' to access these contemporary exemplary speakers.

3.1. Hebrew Grammarians

Among the Hebrew grammarians, the one group that constitutes a reliable body of contemporary exemplary speakers is that of the Tiberian Masoretes and, at least in some cases from an ideological perspective, the commonfolk of the city of Tiberias as well.[39]

3.1.1. ʿEli ben Yehudah ha-Nazir (10th c. CE)

As Drory (2000, 141) points out, the special status afforded to the Tiberian reading tradition and the Tiberian Masoretes seems to have been (at least ideologically) transferred to the people of the city of Tiberias as well. This association of linguistic eloquence with the common population of Tiberias is perhaps most clear from a fragmentary Judeo-Arabic text attributed to a tenth-century Hebrew grammarian known as ʿEli ben Yehudah ha-Nazir (10th c. CE). This fragment, published by Allony, includes an account of this scholar attempting to verify the proper pronunciation of the Hebrew letter *resh*. After thorough textual study and observation of contemporary language 'use', he ventures to the city of Tiberias to hear the 'pure' speech of its inhabitants (Allony 1970, 98–100; Drory 2000, 138–41):

> פאטלת אלענאיה ואלבחת׳ ואק[מ]ת אבח[ת׳] אל קראן וכלאם
> אלאסתעמאל פכ׳רג בעד תעב טויל וענא שדיד פאמתחנת וׄעארצֿת בד׳לך
> פי ג׳מיע אל קראן ופי אלכלאם אלמסתעמל וכנת אטיל אלג׳לוס פי
> סאחאת טבריהׄ ושוארעהא א[סת]מע כלאם אלסוקה ואלעאמה ואבחת׳

---

[39] This section is largely based on the work of Drory (2000, 139–42).

עןׄ אללגה ואצול[הא] אנטׄר הל ינכסר שי ממא אצלת או ינפסד שי ממא
טׄהר לי ופי מא נֻטק ב[ה מן] אלעבראני ואל סריאני ואנואעה אעׄ לגה
אלתרגום וגירה פאנה מג׳אנס ללעבראני כמא [ד׳כרת] אנׄפא פי אלפן
אל[י]ב פכ׳רג׳ צחיח מחרר[40]

I have spent a lot of time considering and researching [this issue of the *resh*]. I conducted a search in the Bible and colloquial speech (*kalām al-istiʿmāl*; lit.: 'speech of use'). Eventually, after long toil and great trouble it came out [clear]. I checked and compared [my findings] in this matter with [Hebrew usage] in all the Bible and in colloquial speech (*al-kalām al-mustaʿmal*; lit.: 'speech in use'). I would spend long periods sitting in the squares and streets of Tiberias, listening to the speech of the commonfolk and the general populace (*kalām al-sūqa wa-l-ʿāmma*) while making enquiries into the language and its rules to see if anything I had set down as a rule was proven wrong or if anything that had occurred to me was shown to be mistaken [when compared] with what is uttered in Hebrew or various forms of Aramaic, that is, the language of the *Targum* and other kinds, for it is related to Hebrew, as I have already mentioned earlier in the twelfth chapter. And [all my findings] have turned out to be completely accurate.

According to Drory (2000, 138–41), this passage appears to reflect a sort of 'fieldwork' motif or *topos*. The grammarian must

40 ≈ فأطلت العناية والبحث وأقمت أبحث القرآن وكلام الاستعمال فخرج بعد تعب طويل وعناء شديد فامتحنت وعارضت بذلك في جميع القرآن وفي الكلام المستعمل وكنت أطيل الجلوس في ساحات طبرية وشوارعها أستمع كلام السوقة والعامة وأبحث عن اللغة وأصولها أنظر هل ينكسر شيء مما أصلت أو ينفسد شيء مما ظهر لي وفي ما نُطق به من العبراني والسرياني وأنواعه أعني لغة الترجوم وغيره فإنه مجانس للعبراني كما ذكرت آنفا في الفن ال-١٢. فخرج صحيح محرر

venture out to hear the pure unadulterated speech of a particular group of exemplary speakers. According to Khan (2020, I:2–3, 118–19), however, references to the speech of the people of Tiberias here are unlikely to refer to colloquial language. It is more likely the case that ʿEli ben Yehudah ha-Nazir was listening to Hebrew in a liturgical context and/or a 'Hebrew component' in the vernacular (Aramaic?) of the Tiberian population.

The explanations of Drory and Khan, however, are not mutually exclusive. Whatever it was precisely that he was hearing in Tiberias, the fact that he ventured there at all to listen to the people on the streets betrays an underlying ideology. Indeed, even if this story recounts a careful analysis of liturgical Hebrew and/or the Hebrew component of colloquial Aramaic, it is still ideologically cast in such a way so as to elevate the linguistic behaviour of the commonfolk of the city of Tiberias. It is, of course, also possible that this portion of the narrative (or the way in which it is framed) is merely an ideological construct, in which case its relevance for the present discussion is apparent.

3.1.2. David ben Abraham al-Fāsī (10th c. CE)

Although the preceding passage may provide us with the best example of linguistic eloquence being ascribed to the commonfolk of Tiberias, similar sentiments are attested among other medieval Hebrew grammarians as well. Note, for example, the explanation that David ben Abraham al-Fāsī (10th c. CE) provides in his lexicon for the phrase אמרי שפר *ʾimrē šɔ̄fɛr* 'sayings of beauty', which occurs in Jacob's blessing of his son Naphtali (Gen. 49.21; Skoss 1936–1945, II:699; Drory 2000, 141):

> הנׄתן אמרי שֶׁפר אקאויל חסנׄה וכׄץ בדׄלך אהל טבריה והו חסן אללגׄה ואלמנטק[41]
>
> *hannōθēn ʾimrē šɔ̄fɛr*: [This means] 'beautiful sayings'. The people of Tiberias are special in this, namely beauty of language and speech.

While it is well known that the Tiberian tradition was regarded as the most prestigious reading tradition of the Middle Ages, the transference of this ideology to the population of the city is noteworthy. Though the point is somewhat speculative, this phenomenon of transference (see chapter 3, §2.2) may provide some insight into processes of enregisterment current among the medieval Jewish community. The prestigious reading of the Hebrew Bible was the preserve of an elite group of scholars, known as the Tiberian Masoretes, who happened to work in Tiberias. In reality, the preservation of the reading tradition was due to their scholarly heritage and erudition, rather than their geographical residence in Tiberias. Nevertheless, as we described earlier (chapter 3, §2.2), the intersection of different social types can sometimes lead to different configurations of enregisterment. A passage like this may reveal that some members of the Jewish community enregistered the exemplary language of the Tiberian reading tradition to the geographical place rather than to the prestigious scholarly background of the Tiberian Masoretes. Whether we refer to this as transference or enregisterment, in one way or another the linguistic reputation of this elite group of scholars was extended to the city itself.

---

41 ≈ הנׄתן אמרי שֶׁפר: أقاويل حسنة وخصّ بذلك أهل طبريّة وهو حسن اللغة والمنطق.

3.1.3. Jonah ibn Janāḥ (ca 990–ca 1050 CE)

A similar esteem for the speech of the Tiberians—as already pointed out by Drory—is also attested in Jonah ibn Janāḥ's (ca 990–ca 1050 CE) *Kitāb al-lumaʿ*. When referring to أهل طبرية 'the people of Tiberias', he writes the following (Derenbourg 1886, 29; Drory 2000, 141):

אד הם אפצח אלעבראניין לסאנא ואכת̇רהם ביאנא[42]

> As they (i.e., the people of Tiberias) are the most eloquent of the Hebrews in language and the best of them in communication.

It is not entirely clear here whether Ibn Janāḥ has in mind the Tiberian Masoretes or the general population of the city of Tiberias itself. In either case, this passage appears to provide further support for the idea that the prestige of the Tiberian tradition was at least somewhat associated with geography or demographics. Once again, this may reflect the dynamicity of enregisterment, through which the linguistic signs of the tradition might be enregistered to the geographical place rather than to the scholarly profile of its tradents. Although we do not have access to the social contexts in which such enregisterment might have taken place, we can speculate that tradents of the Tiberian reading tradition—depending on the social clues they presented—might just as easily have been associated with the city of Tiberias rather than specifically with the circle of elite scholars who carried out their work there. Alternatively, we may suggest that our framework of transference might also apply here. Due to limited access

---

[42] ≈ إذ هم أفصح العبرانيين لسانا وأكثرهم بيانا.

to the Tiberian Masoretes and the commonfolk of Tiberias among the wider Jewish community, the linguistic signs associated with the more limited group of scholars were transferred (in their perceived association) to the wider demographic of Tiberian residents.

3.1.4. Abū al-Faraj Hārūn ibn al-Faraj (first half of 11th c. CE)

Abū al-Faraj Hārūn (first half of 11th c. CE) similarly imputes a distinct and prestigious pronunciation of *resh* to those living in Tiberias, even attributing their unique pronunciation to the climate of the town (Khan 2020, II.L.1.9.3):

> ואעלם אן אלטבראניין דכרו אן להם ריש לא יקראה גירהם ואלקריב אן הוא בלדהם יפעלה[43]
>
> And know that the Tiberians have mentioned that they have a *resh* that no one else reads the way they do. It is likely that it is the climate of their town that makes it so.

Attributing this particular pronunciation to הוא בלדהם (≈ هواء بلدهم) 'the climate of their town' demonstrates that the physical geography itself had come to take on a special status and not just the scholarly circle working there. This could actually constitute a fairly classic example of enregisterment in which a particular linguistic feature, in this case the unique pronunciation of *resh*, indexes a place, in this case the city of Tiberias (see chapter 3, §2.2). We might imagine how, when heard 'live', a biblical reading with such a *resh* by one introduced as belonging to *ahl*

---

[43] ≈ واعلم أن الطبرانيين ذكروا أن لهم ריש لا يقرأه غيرهم والقريب أن هواء بلدهم يفعله.

ṭabariyya might serve to enregister such a feature as 'Tiberian' for the hearers. If such an example constitutes a microcosm of a wider societal belief common among the Jewish community, then we might even speculate that those who implemented features of the Masoretic reading tradition in their biblical recitation and/or performances sounded (demographically or geographically) 'Tiberian' to their hearers.

3.2. Comparison with the Arabic Tradition

As is well known, Arabic literature is rife with examples of grammarians and poets seeking the help of Bedouin informants as sources of pure and eloquent Arabic. This trope—more of a construct than objective reality—involves going out into the desert to conduct 'fieldwork' and retrieve linguistic examples from the Bedouin. These stories were intended to bolster the prestige of the researchers (Brustad 2016, 152). Indeed, at least among the later grammarians, the Bedouin of the desert have come to be regarded as the best contemporary source of pure and unadulterated *ʿarabiyya.*

3.2.1. al-Akhfaš al-Awsaṭ (d. 830 CE)

Though more characteristic of later (ninth- and tenth-century) grammarians, the esteem of the grammarians for the language of *al-aʿrāb* 'the Bedouin' might already be seen to some degree in al-Akhfaš's (d. 830 CE) *Kitāb al-qawāfī*. In the opening, when attempting to define the concept of a *qāfiya* 'rhyme' (Drory 2000, 81), he notes that he conferred with a Bedouin (ʿIzzat 1970, 2):

وقد يجعلُ بعضُهم القافيةَ كَلِمَتَيْنِ. سألتُ أعرابياً، وأنشد

> ...and some of them might make the rhyme two words. I asked a Bedouin (*aʿrābī*) and he recited [a line of poetry]...

This passage may already hint at the role of the Bedouin in determining the correctness of poetic verses. At the same time, however, the full-fledged ideology of the 'pure' language of the Bedouin in the desert had not yet developed.

3.2.2. al-Jāḥiẓ (d. 868/869 CE)

More significant for the present discussion, however, is the *topos* of various poets going out to the desert to pick up pure *ʿarabiyya* from the Bedouin. Al-Jāḥiẓ (d. 868/869 CE), for example, the famous and prolific prose author and philologist (among other things) from Baṣra, recounts an instance of Abū Nuwās going to al-Mirbad to find a Bedouin informant (*al-Ḥayawān*, 6.441; al-Sūd 2003; van Gelder 1997, 281):

وحدثني أبو نُواس قال: بكرتُ إلى المِربَد، ومعي ألواحي أطلبُ أعرابيًّا فصيحًا، فإذا في ظلِّ دار جعفر أعرابيٌّ لم أسمع بشيطان أقبَحَ منه وجهًا، ولا بإنسان أحسنَ منه عقلا

> Abū Nuwās told me, "I went out early in the morning to al-Mirbad with my [writing] tablets in hand seeking a Bedouin speaking pure Arabic. And, sure enough, in the shade of Jaʿfar's house was a Bedouin, uglier-in-face than any devil I've ever heard of, but better-in-intellect than any man I've ever known."

Al-Mirbad, which was just outside the city of Baṣra, symbolised a sort of mediating area (geographically, culturally, socially, economically, etc.) between the urban and the rural. Apparently, it was not uncommon for poets and philologists from the city to be described as seeking the aid of eloquent Bedouin there (van Gelder 1997, 281–82). It is said elsewhere of Abū Nuwās, in fact, that he spent an entire year in the desert with the Bedouin to take in their purity of language and obscure vocabulary (Al-ʿAzzāwī 1978, 39; Alqarni 2014, 65).

Al-Jāḥiẓ actually appears to have had a prominent role in developing this ideal. According to Webb (2016, 297–99), al-Jāḥiẓ does this by converting what was formerly just a spatial boundary (between the urban and the rural) into a linguistic one, especially in his book *Al-bayān wa-l-tabyīn*. This is perhaps most apparent in his description of a certain poet's house as located at موضع الفصاحة 'the last place of clear/eloquent speech' and موضع العجمة 'the first place of improper speech'. Moreover, while he describes the city as a force for the corruption of the language, the desert is depicted as the source of pure Arabic. In one instance in *Al-bayān wa-l-tabyīn*, this purity of language appears to be attributed at least in part to the geography (1.163; Haroun 1998; Webb 2016, 297–98):

> لأنّ تلك اللُّغَةَ إنّما انقادت واستوت، واطّردت وتكاملت، بالخصال التى اجتمعت لها فى تلك الجزيرة [وفى تلك الجيرة]، ولفقد الخطاءِ من جميع الأمم
>
> For that language (i.e., Arabic) only runs properly, remains level, flows continuously, and reaches perfection by virtue of the conditions which come together for it in that Peninsula (*jazīra*) and between its neighbours (*jīra*), and because of the lack of [linguistic] error [in the area] from all the peoples (*umam*) (i.e., those with improper speech).

This attribution of linguistic purity—at least in part—to geographical features is reminiscent of some of the descriptions of Tiberias and the linguistic purity of the Tiberians noted above. It should also be noted that this pattern of going out into the desert to do 'fieldwork' is evidenced in a number of other Arabic philologists over the following century.[44]

3.2.3. al-Waššāʾ (d. 936/937 CE)

We might also note that in his treatise on Arabic rhetoric entitled *Kitāb al-fāḍil fī ṣifat al-adab al-kāmil*, al-Waššāʾ (ca 936/937 CE), a grammarian and lexicographer of Baghdad, describes a number of instances in which *al-aʿrāb* 'the Bedouin' seem to interject poetic verses into everyday conversation.[45] Note the following example (al-Ǧabūrī 1991, 173):

كنا في حَلْقَة يونس النحوي، فجاء أعرابيان فوقفا علينا فسلَّما، ثم قال أحدهما: إنّ الدنيا دار فناء، والآخرة دار بقاء

> When we were in the circle of Yūnus the *naḥwī*, two Bedouin (*aʿrābiyyān*) came, stood by us, and greeted us. Then one of them said, "The world is a house destined for extinction (*dār fanāʾ*), and the afterlife is a house destined to remain (*dār baqāʾ*)."

The image of a couple of Bedouin dropping by to greet the grammarian and his circle before erupting into eloquent verse is

[44] E.g., Ibn Durayd (d. 933 CE), al-Azharī (d. 980 CE), Ibn al-Jinnī (d. 1002 CE), and al-Jawharī (d. 1002/1003 CE). See Touati (2010, 67–68).

[45] Such examples are also referred to by Drory (2000, 35).

almost as comical as it is striking. Nevertheless, it clearly demonstrates how highly regarded they were for their language prowess, especially in poetry.

3.2.4. al-Zubaydī (d. 989 CE)

We also see a similar esteem for the Bedouin in some of the later biographies about Sībawayh, in which his dispute with the grammarians in Baghdad involves a Bedouin settling linguistic questions. Al-Zubaydī (d. 989 CE), the Andalusian scholar known for his biographies of philologists, recounts the story in *Ṭabaqāt al-naḥwiyyīn wa-l-lughawiyyīn* (Ibrāhīm 1973, 68) as follows (Brustad 2016, 160):

> فسألوه: كيف تقول: «كنت أظن العقرب أشدَّ لَسْعَةً من الزُّنْبور فإذا هو هى» أو «هو إياها»؟ قال: أقول: «فإذا هو هى». فأقبل عليه الجميع فقالوا: أخطأت ولحنْتَ. فقال يحيى بن خالد بن برمك: هذا موضعٌ مُشْكِل؛ حتى يُحْكَم بينكم، فقالوا: هؤلاء الأعراب على الباب؛ فأدخل أبو الجرّاح ومَنْ وُجد معه ممّن كان يأخذ منهُ الكسائىّ وأصحابُه. فقالوا: «فإذا هو إياها»

> And they (i.e., al-Kisāʾī, al-Farrāʾ, al-Aḥmar, et al.) asked him, “How do you say, ‘I used to think that the scorpion was stronger in bite than the wasp, but they are alike (*fa-iḏā huwa hiya*),’ or [should you say], ‘*huwa iyyāhā*’?” He said, “I say, *fa-iḏā huwa hiya*.” And everyone approached him and said, “You have erred and spoken ungrammatically.” And Yaḥyā ibn Khālid ibn Barmak said, “This is a difficult situation so as to be judged between you.” And they said, “Those Bedouin are at the door.” And Abū al-Jarrāḥ was brought in along with those who were with him from among those who served al-Kisāʾī and his companions, and they said, “*fa-iḏā huwa iyyāhā*.”

In this passage, al-Zubaydī describes the Bedouin as the *par excellence* linguistic informants for the *ʿarabiyya*. It is especially noteworthy that even in a setting like this, in the presence of some of the most preeminent names in Arabic grammar, the Bedouin are still regarded as the most authoritative source for determining proper Arabic.

3.2.5. al-Jawharī (d. 1002/1003 CE)

Finally, we may also note that the Persian lexicographer al-Jawharī (d. 1002/1003 CE) introduces his methods in his dictionary as follows (*al-Ṣiḥāḥ*, 1.33; ʿAṭṭār 1984):

> أما بعد فإنى قد أودعت هذا الكتاب ما صَحَّ عندى من هذه اللغة... فى ثمانية وعشرين بابًا، وكل باب منها ثمانية وعشرون فصلا: على عدد حروف المُعْجَم وترتِيبها، إلَّا أن يُهمَل من الأبواب جنسٌ من الفصول؛ بعد تحصيلها بالعراق رواية، وإتقانها دراية، ومشافهتى بها العرب العاربة، فى ديارهم بالبادية
>
> Now, I have endowed this book with what I have regarded as correct from this language... in twenty-eight chapters, each of which has twenty-eight sections: According to the number of letters of the dictionary and their arrangement, lest a particular type of section be neglected from the chapters, after acquiring [the language] in Iraq by oral transmission (*riwāya*), gaining mastery of it by personal reflection (*dirāya*), and using it in oral exchange (*mušāfaha*) with the 'true' Arabs (*al-ʿarab al-ʿāriba*) in their abodes in the desert (*al-bādiya*).[46]

As is clear from this telling comment in his introduction, al-Jawharī and many other philologists regarded the desert as

---

[46] Translation in consultation with Touati (2010, 68).

"their field of investigation" (Touati 2010, 76).[47] Because of the generally inaccessible nature of this field, however, the role of the grammarian in exerting the necessary (painstaking) effort to acquire the language is all the more important.

3.3. Analysis

In both the Hebrew and Arabic grammatical traditions, then, the *contemporary* locus of pure language comes to reside in a very specific and 'distant' segment of the population. In the Arabic grammatical tradition, this group is comprised of the Bedouin, whose habitation is in the desert. Because of this, grammarians and poets must venture out of the city into the desert to conduct 'fieldwork' among Bedouin informants. While this literary *topos* is much less developed in the Hebrew tradition, the account of ʿEli ben Yehudah ha-Nazir doing 'fieldwork' in Tiberias to check the proper pronunciation of *resh* seems at least in part influenced by such an ideological *topos*. At least for him, it was the Tiberian Masoretes and thus also the population of Tiberias that constituted the contemporary locus of pure language.[48]

---

[47] Al-Aṣmaʿī in particular appears to have been known as a regular frequenter of the desert for Bedouin informants (Blachère 1950, 46).

[48] Note that a similar theme is also echoed in a Hebrew treatise about *resh*, in which the commonfolk of Tiberias are credited with a particular pronunciation: והוא קשור בלשונם אם יקראו במקרא ואם ישיחו בשיחתם והוא בפי האנשים והנשים ובפי הטף *v-hū qɔ̄ʃūr bi-lʃōnɔ̄m ʾim yiqrʾū bam-miqrɔ̄ v-ʾim yɔ̄sīḥū b-sīḥɔ̄θɔ̄m v-hū b-fī hɔ̄-ʾanɔ̄ʃīm v-han-nɔ̄ʃīm u-v-fī haṭ-ṭaf* 'it is on their tongues, whether they read the Bible or converse in their conversation, in the mouths of men, women and children' (Baer and Strack 1879, §7; Khan 2020, I:119).

What is especially significant about all these references and literary *topoi* in the Arabic tradition, however, is that their nature appears to change over time. This is, at least in part, due to the semantic and cultural evolution of the term *ʿarab* and the concept of 'Arabness' in the society at large. In an earlier period—i.e., that of al-Khalīl and Sībawayh—the group known as *al-ʿarab* was linguistically defined, simply referring to those belonging to the speech community of pure Arabic, whether those engaged in performance or merely reliable speakers of *al-ʿarabiyya* (for more on this debate, see the discussion in §2.2.1). Though the Bedouin could be part of this group, they were by no means synonymous with it in this early period. We do not find accounts of early grammarians like Sībawayh going out into the desert to confer with the Bedouin. By the ninth and tenth centuries, however, the term becomes more ethnically imbued, so that *kalām al-ʿarab*, in addition to its earlier signification of the corpus of *al-ʿarabiyya*, also comes to connote 'speech of the Arabs (= Bedouin)'. Part of this shift was likely also due to the ever-increasing divide between urban and rural life (Gouttenoire 2006, 45–46, 54; Brustad 2016, 151–53)[49] as well as the 'Bedouinisation' of the term *ʿarab*—and the concept of 'Arabness' generally—throughout this period (Webb 2016, 294–351).

It should also be noted that the ideology here must differ somewhat from the reality. While it is true that those living in rural areas tend to maintain a more conservative form of the language, these depictions appear to betray something of ideological

[49] For more on the 'fieldwork' *topos*, see Blachère (1950); Touati (2010, §2); Brustad (2016, 151–53).

embellishment. This is especially the case as time goes on and even the speech of the Bedouin is several centuries removed from that of the *Qurʾān* and pre-Islamic poetry.

While the general parallel between the two traditions with respect to the 'fieldwork' *topos* has been pointed out in previous scholarship—most notably Drory (2000, 141–42)—there are a few layers of sociolinguistic significance that have yet to be fully explored. In the preceding two sections (§§1.0–2.0), we discussed the tension between the grammarians regarding their language as a 'cultural possession', on the one hand, while still presenting it as something external to contemporary speakers, on the other. One way of doing so was by placing the locus of pure language and its exemplary speakers *chronologically* in the distant past.

The 'fieldwork' *topos*, on the other hand, places the locus of pure language and its exemplary speakers *demographically* and/or *geographically* among a limited segment of the population even if in the present, namely the Bedouin of the desert in the Arabic tradition and the Tiberian Masoretes (and Tiberian population) in the Hebrew tradition. In this way, the language is still regarded as a cultural possession but one well out of reach for most of the population—apart from significant training. While the general population are disconnected from the exemplary speakers of the past by an insurmountable chronological gap, they are also separated from the exemplary speakers of the present by a highly challenging geographical (and/or demographic) expanse.[50] Nevertheless, while the inaccessible speakers of the past strengthen the role and prestige of the scholar, the somewhat more accessible (even if with difficulty) speakers of the present provide a historic or geographic link, and in so doing represent a link with the past. In a way, both the exemplary speakers of the past and those of the present serve to reinforce the standard language ideology, namely the idea that the language has a correct form that exists beyond most speakers. It is not what is already familiar to most speakers (see chapter 3, §2.1.3).

It is for this reason that the grammarian's role as language documentor and evaluator becomes all the more important. Just as the grammarian must search out ancient texts for linguistic examples, so too must he venture out into the desert (or Tiberias) to retrieve pure language from the exemplary speakers. In this way, the grammarian bridges the gap between the exemplary speakers and the general population. Rather, he does the work of bringing the best exemplary speakers to the general population.

This sort of 'fieldwork', however, is not merely a neutral activity of a disinterested observer. By affirming the linguistic purity of the Bedouin or the Tiberians, the grammarians are not merely reflecting an existing language ideology but helping to shape it as well. In elevating the linguistic behaviour of these groups—alongside the more ancient corpora of pure language—the grammarians implicitly present them (i.e., the Bedouin and

[50] Note that there does seem to have been a social barrier between the general populace and the Tiberian Masoretes, given that they were an elite circle of scholars.

Tiberians) as the heirs of the inheritance that is the ancient sacred language. This act of historicisation serves to reinforce a continuum that connects the ancient exemplary speakers to their contemporary counterparts (see chapter 3, §2.1.8).

Finally, it is also worth noting that both traditions exhibit something of a shift in how the contemporary group of exemplary speakers was regarded. In the earliest stages of the Arabic grammatical tradition, the exemplary speakers were not necessarily 'Bedouin' but merely those among the Arabic speech community with the most trustworthy and pleasing form of Arabic, whether those actively engaged and most proficient in the performance language culture of *kalām* or simply those judged speakers of pure Arabic for other reasons (for more on this debate, see the discussion in §2.2.1). It was only at a later stage that this idea came to be transferred demographically or geographically to ethnic Bedouin of the desert. Similarly, ʿEli ben Yehudah ha-Nazir, at least in his ideological presentation, appears to transfer some of the linguistic authority of the elite group of scholars known as the Tiberian Masoretes demographically or geographically to the general population of Tiberias. In fact, various grammarians of each tradition even ascribe the credit for the purity of the language to the physical geography of the locales in which it is spoken. Abū al-Faraj credits the unique and proper speech of the Tiberians to הוא בלדהם (≈ هواء بلدهم) 'the climate of their town' and al-Jāḥiẓ claims that the Arabic of the Arabian Peninsula reaches perfection بالخصال التي اجتمعت لها في تلك الجزيرة 'by virtue of the conditions which come together for it in that Peninsula (*jazīra*)'.

Such processes of transference become integral parts of how speakers (and/or language users) represent and embody attitudes and beliefs about language in the Hebrew and Arabic grammatical traditions. Though perhaps beyond what we as moderns can access, they might also have become integral parts of the processes of enregisterment involved in the development of the respective standard language ideologies. At least theoretically, we can surmise that reciting the Hebrew Bible in the Masoretic tradition might have made someone sound (geographically or demographically) 'Tiberian'. Similarly, flawless proficiency in the *ʿarabiyya* might have conjured up associations with the 'Bedouin' population of the desert.

5. THE PURPOSE OF THE STANDARD LANGUAGE AND THE GRAMMARIANS' MISSION

In a way, the three features of similarity covered in the preceding chapter dealt with the definition, corpus, and sources of the standard canonical language. Beginning here, however, we turn to similarities in the (standard) language ideology of the Hebrew and Arabic grammarians related to the practical use of the language in society and the ultimate purposes of their work in and for their own time and culture.

1.0. Performative Language: خطبهم وأشعارهم

Even though the pool of exemplary speakers of pure Hebrew and Arabic was confined to ancient sources—or small segments of the contemporary population like the Tiberians or the Bedouin—this did not stop the grammarians' contemporaries from emulating the linguistic eloquence of these 'ancient' speakers in their own time. In fact, it seems that, in each tradition, the grammarians were at least ideologically concerned with providing instruction in how to contemporaneously perform in a formal and prescribed way with the appropriate register of the language.

1.1. Hebrew Grammarians

Even though the Hebrew grammarians were primarily occupied with describing the language of the Bible so that their audience

 https://doi.org/10.11647/OBP.0382.05

could read and understand it, there are hints that they were also concerned, at least to some degree, with real productive use of the standard language, albeit in performance contexts.

1.1.1. Saadia Gaon (882–942 CE)

In *Sefer Ha-Egron* (44–45; Harkavy 1891), for example, while lamenting the poor Hebrew abilities of the nation, Saadia (882–942 CE) points to several spheres of language use in which the people are lacking in proficiency:

> ואד̇א הם תכלמו כאן כת̇ירא ממא ילפט̇ון בה מלחונא ואד̇א הם שערו
> כאן אלמסתפיץ̇ פי מא בינהם מן אלארכאן אלאואיל הו אלקליל
> ואלמתרוך הו אכת̇ר: וכד̇לך פי אלקואפי חתי צאר אלכתאב נפסה ענדהם
> כאלגאמץ̇ מן אלכלאם ואלג̇בי מן אלקול[48]
>
> When they speak (*takallamū*), much of what they utter is grammatically wrong (*malḥūn*). When they compose and recite poetry (*šaʿarū*), that which spreads among them from the ancient foundations (i.e., the poetic rules) is little, and that which is abandoned [so that it is not governed by these rules] is more. And so it is in [their] rhymes, such that the book itself (i.e., the Bible) has become like something obscure to them with respect to [its] idiom (*kalām*) or [like] a collection of sayings [without any connection].

Although Saadia mentions various spheres of language use for the purpose of upbraiding the people, the contexts in which

---

48 ≈ وإذا هم تكلموا كان كثيرا مما يلفظون به ملحونا وإذا هم شعروا كان المستفيض في ما بينهم من الأركان الأوائل هو القليل والمتروك هو أكثر. وكذلك في القوافي حتى صار الكتاب نفسه عندهم كالغامض من الكلام والجبى من القول.

the people are said to fail in their attempt at (re)producing eloquent Hebrew actually reveal lively and dynamic linguistic activity. First, they are prone to err when they speak (ואדׄא הם תכלמו ≈ وإذا هم تكلموا). Presumably, this does not refer to everyday speech in the marketplace but to public orations (perhaps in liturgical contexts) and the like. Second, when they compose and recite poetry (ואדׄא הם שערו ≈ وإذا هم شعروا), they veer from the rules established by the ancient poets. Apparently, instead of replicating the language patterns of the 'ancients' (i.e., biblical authors and *payṭanim*), they produce a different sort of linguistic style not governed by such rules. Like speeches, the composition and recitation of Hebrew poetry was presumably a formal public (and possibly liturgical) activity. In any case, as a result of this lack of Hebrew proficiency, evidenced by the failure to produce proper Hebrew when delivering speeches or reciting poetry in formal contexts, the *kalām* of the Bible has become unintelligible to them.[49]

As we have already hinted at earlier, the particular spheres of language use that Saadia has in mind are modes of speaking that may be regarded as performance. While the fact that the people were productively using Hebrew to compose and recite poetry may not be a surprise—we touched on this earlier (see

---

49 Note, however, that Saadia refers to speaking Hebrew in the Hebrew introduction to *Sefer Ha-Egron* (Harkavy 1891, 52–57). This may reflect something of an ideology of wanting to restore Hebrew even as a common everyday language. Nevertheless, despite this ideological desire, the settings he is describing in this passage do not fit such a context.

chapter 4, §2.1.3)—the precise meaning of ואדֹא הם תכלמו (≈ وإذا هم تكلموا) 'and when they speak…' might be more elusive. Since Hebrew was no longer an everyday vernacular in the Middle Ages (Sáenz-Badillos 2013), we must infer that 'speaking' here refers to some kind of public speech. This inference is perhaps made clearer by a passage in Ḥayyūj (see §1.1.2).

1.1.2. Judah ben David Ḥayyūj (945–1000 CE)

Indeed, insight into the nature of what such 'speaking' in Hebrew entailed at the time of the Hebrew grammarians may be hinted at in Ḥayyūj's (945–1000 CE) comments in the introduction to his book on the morphology of weak verbs, *Kitāb al-afʿāl ḏawāt ḥurūf al-līn* (Jastrow 1897, 1):

> فقد خَفِيَ امرُها عن كثير من الناس لِلينها واعتلالها ودقّة معانيها وبُعد غورها فلا يدرون كيف تتصرّف الافعال ذوات حُرُوف اللين وكثيرا ما يستعملونها فى خُطَبِهِمْ واشعارهم على غَيْرِ ٱلصّواب
>
> And the matter of [the conjugation of weak verbs] has been hidden from many of the people with respect to their weakness, defectiveness, precise meanings, and the extent of their declivity, so that they do not know how weak verbs conjugate and they frequently use them (*yastaʿmilūnahā*) in their speeches (*fī ḫuṭabihim*) and their poems (*ašʿārihim*) in an incorrect manner (*ʿalā ghayr al-ṣawāb*).

In this passage Ḥayyūj is highlighting a linguistic problem. The people are not able to correctly conjugate weak verbs. As was the case with the passage in Saadia's *Sefer Ha-Egron*, there are two contexts in which this problem is prevalent: في خطبهم 'in their speeches' and في... أشعارهم 'in their poems'. The fact that Ḥayyūj explicitly uses the term *ḫuṭab* 'speeches; orations' helps clarify what Saadia meant by ואדא הם תכלמו (≈ وإذا هم تكلموا) 'and when they speak...'. Both grammarians are probably referring to some sort of formal orations or public speeches. Such speeches were probably of a religious and/or pedagogical nature and delivered within the context of the synagogue or educational institutions.[50]

We should reiterate here that everyday spoken language is not necessarily what the Hebrew grammarians are addressing; Hebrew had not been used that way for hundreds of years. Rather, they are trying to prepare the people to produce correct Hebrew specifically in performance settings. This is because, for the Hebrew grammarians and their contemporaries, *lughat al-ʿibrāniyyīn* 'the language of the Hebrews' was immediately experienced as a performance language in public recitation of the Bible, liturgical poetry, religious speeches, etc. At the same time, however, there seems to have been an ideological undercurrent among at least some grammarians who wanted to restore Hebrew as an everyday spoken language. This seems to be evidenced to some degree in Saadia's Hebrew introduction to *Sefer Ha-Egron* (Harkavy 1891, 52–57) and in the works of the Karaite scholar

---

[50] Medieval Hebrew was not a language used for everyday communication. Nevertheless, some Jewish communities had maintained Hebrew in written and spoken forms, largely within the context of the synagogue and educational institutions (Sáenz-Badillos 2013).

Benjamin al-Nahāwandī (9th c. CE).[51] Nevertheless, just because some advocated for using Hebrew as an everyday spoken language, does not mean that this practice was particularly common. While it is possible that the grammarians were rebuking mistakes among those trying to use Hebrew for everyday conversation, it is perhaps more plausible that their rebukes apply specifically to performative contexts.

1.2. Comparison with the Arabic Tradition

As we have already hinted at in preceding sections, the Arabic terms *kalām al-ʿarab* and *al-ʿarabiyya* refer to the corpus and particular register (or variety) of the standard language, respectively. It should additionally be noted that, though perhaps not universally in all the Arabic grammarians, there is a strong correlation between these terms and the performance register of Arabic as well. Since we have already dealt with this topic extensively as it applies to the term *kalām al-ʿarab* earlier (see chapter 4, §2.2), we will focus more on the term *al-ʿarabiyya* here.

According to Brustad (2016, 149–51), in the grammars of al-Khalīl (d. 786/791 CE) and Sībawayh (d. ca 796 CE), the feminine singular adjectival form *al-ʿarabiyya* is always used as a noun. As such, it contrasts with the *Qurʾānic* term *lisān ʿarabī* 'Arabic language' both in definiteness and in its use as a substantive. The *tāʾ marbūṭa* at the end of *al-ʿarabiyya* is probably best regarded as an abstract noun marker.[52] The term thus refers to the

---

[51] Personal communication from Geoffrey Khan.

[52] This is more likely than the possibility that *al-ʿarabiyya* is a feminine adjective referring to an implied omitted noun like *lugha*—i.e., *al-lugha*

abstract language and/or language register reflected in the *kalām al-ʿarab* corpus. Specifically, then, it refers to an elevated performance register of Arabic.[53] This is consistent with the fact that the earliest grammarians were concerned primarily with the performed recitation of the *Qurʾān*.

It should be noted, however, that even at an early period, namely that of al-Khalīl and Sībawayh, *al-ʿarabiyya* was neither a monolith nor identical with the Arabic of the *Qurʾān*. In a comment about Ḥimyar, Ibn Sallām (d. 845/846 CE) notes that ما لسان حِمْيَرَ وأقاصِي اليَمَن بلساننا ولا عربيّتُهم بِعربيّتنا 'the language of Ḥimyar and the remotest parts of Yemen is not our language and their *ʿarabiyya* is not our *ʿarabiyya*' (*Ṭabaqāt fuḥūl al-šuʿarāʾ*; Ibrāhīm 2001, 1.29). As Brustad (2016, 149) points out, implicit in Ibn Sallām's statement is an acknowledgement that various communities had differences both in their specific corpus of the performance register and in the nature of the linguistic register used in the performance of such genres. Van Putten (2022, 47–98), similarly, highlights the linguistic diversity evidenced in what may be termed *al-ʿarabiyya*, even in the early grammarians like Sībawayh and al-Farrāʾ. Finally, we should also note that, even if we subscribe to the view that *al-ʿarabiyya* was not exclusively a performance register but could admit some colloquial dialectal

---

al-ʿarabiyya—which still meant '(dialect) variant' in this early period (Brustad 2016, 149).

[53] As Brustad points out, there are several statements among the early Arabic grammarians that make a distinction between 'language' and *al-ʿarabiyya* or between 'grammar' and *al-ʿarabiyya* (Brustad 2016, 149).

forms, as claimed by Webb (see discussion in chapter 4, §2.2.1), the *ʿarabiyya* was at least strongly associated with or most clearly exemplified in 'texts' that were orally performed in formal contexts.

Although there are many sources within the Arabic grammatical tradition that highlight the performative nature (or associations) of *al-ʿarabiyya*, we focus below on just one in particular that exhibits similar phraseology to the Hebrew grammarians examined above as it relates to the association of the standard language with reciting poetry and delivering public orations.

1.2.1. al-Khalīl ibn Aḥmad (d. 786/791 CE)

Al-Khalīl (d. 786/791 CE), after noting in the opening of *Kitāb al-ʿayn* that the scope of his work includes *kalām al-ʿarab*, outlines his purposes in writing his dictionary. These may be generally summed up as helping the Arabs improve their familiarity with and competence in their linguistic heritage. What is noteworthy in his description of his goals for the Arabs who read his book, however, is how the particular genres of language use mentioned by al-Khalīl bear a striking resemblance to the spheres of language use mentioned by Saadia and Ḥayyūj in their lamenting the poor proficiency of the people in Hebrew (1.47; al-Makhzūmī and al-Sāmarrāʾī 1989):[54]

هذا ما أَلفه الخليل بن أحمد البصريّ—رحمة اللّه عليه. من حروف: ا، ب،
ت، ث، مع ما تكمَّلَتْ به فكان مدار كلام العرب وألفاظهم. فلا يخرج منها

[54] Brustad (2016, 150) cites this passage as evidence that al-Khalīl associated the *ʿarabiyya* with poetry, proverbs, and formal speeches.

عنه شيء. أراد أن تَعرِفَ به العربُ في أشعارها وأمثالها ومخاطباتها فلا يشِذُّ عنه شَيْء من ذلك

> The following is what al-Khalīl ibn Aḥmad the Baṣran—mercy of God upon him—composed. Of the letters *alif*, *bāʾ*, *tāʾ*, *ṯāʾ*, etc. And the scope of the work was *kalām al-ʿarab* and their words (*alfāẓ*), of which nothing escaped him. His purpose [in writing] was that by means of [his book] the Arabs would become well acquainted with their poems (*ašʿār*), their proverbs (*amṯāl*), and their formal speeches (*muḫāṭabāt*), so that none of it would be beyond its scope.

There are two pieces of evidence in this passage that indicate that al-Khalīl was concerned in *Kitāb al-ʿayn* with documenting the performance register of the language. First, the scope of the work is explicitly defined as *kalām al-ʿarab* (see discussion in chapter 4, §2.2.1). On this point, note that the contents of *Kitāb al-ʿayn* are made up mostly of poetry and the *Qurʾān* (Brustad 2016, 150). Second, the reference to *ašʿār* 'poems', *amṯāl* 'proverbs', and *muḫāṭabāt* 'formal speeches' clearly indicates that al-Khalīl's grammar was occupied with performance settings and/or genres that were orally performed. It is also significant that the purpose of writing his grammar is so that *al-ʿarab* 'the Arabs' would become well acquainted with the linguistic material composed in the performance register. Presumably, this would help better equip them to engage in this performance language culture themselves.[55]

---

[55] Note also the following statement in *Kitāb al-ʿayn* (8.41; al-Makhzūmī and al-Sāmarrāʾī 1989), in which al-Khalīl argues that the word ندل 'filth' does not belong to the linguistic variety under discussion: النَّدْل:

1.3. Analysis

In both the Hebrew and Arabic traditions, we see that the grammarians were not primarily concerned with everyday speech but with an elevated performance register of language. On this point, it is curious that the terms *ḫuṭab* 'speeches' (or *muḫāṭabāt* 'formal speeches') and *aš'ār* 'poems' are repeated in both traditions in close collocations with what is regarded as the standard language the grammarians are endeavouring to document.

From a sociolinguistic or linguistic-anthropological perspective, the rebuke of the people for their inability to speak proper Hebrew reinforces a key element of a standard language ideology, namely that of a pure canonical form of the language existing outside of the practices of native speakers (see chapter 3, §2.1.3). There are thus 'correct' and 'incorrect' forms of the language. Also implicit in such rebukes is the idea that there are contexts in which contemporaries are or should be engaged in this performance language culture. The grammarians thus confer a degree of social prestige on those who exhibit such capabilities. In this way, they engage in a form of 'maintenance' of the standard language (see chapter 3, §2.1.6). By prescribing certain forms of language as proper for performance settings, they also serve

---

الوَسَخُ من كُلِّ شيء من غير استعمال [في العربية] '*Al-nadl:* Filth of every kind. It is not in use in *al-'arabiyya*' (see Brustad 2010). As Brustad (2010) points out, the continued presence of this word in Egyptian Arabic demonstrates that it was clearly in use in Arabic at the time of al-Khalīl. Nevertheless, he does not regard it as belonging to the *'arabiyya*.

the processes of valorisation and circulation (see chapter 3, §§2.2, 3.0).

2.0. Complaint Tradition: توجعت لنسيان الأمة اللغة

Although it was not the focus of the preceding section, one might notice from the statements of Saadia and Ḥayyūj that the Hebrew grammarians tended to view their work as an urgent response to a dire need. In their eyes, the people had neglected and forgotten Hebrew. In a standard language ideology, the idea of grief at the linguistic ineptitude of the masses is what has been termed the 'complaint tradition' (see chapter 3, §§2.1.4–2.1.5). This complaint tradition appears, in many cases, to be the catalyst for the documentation and codification of a standard language by means of grammatical works. Indeed, restoring 'proper' language use after 'corruption' of the language among the masses is often the motivation for writing a grammar. Such a phenomenon appears to be evidenced in both the Hebrew and Arabic grammarians.

2.1. Hebrew Grammarians

Among the Hebrew grammarians, it is not uncommon for the introduction to their works to include an explanation as to their motivation and purposes in writing. In numerous cases, it was the deterioration of the language among the people that drove them to compose their grammatical literature.

2.1.1. Saadia Gaon (882–942 CE)

When offering an explanation in *Sefer Ha-Galuy*[56] as to why he wrote his book on Hebrew poetry (i.e., *Sefer Ha-Egron*), Saadia cites his grief at the nation's forgetting of the Hebrew language (Malter 1913, 494–95, 499; Harkavy 1891, 156–57):

> וכמא שרחת הד̇ה אלג׳ מעאני פי כתאב אלשער אלעבראני פתוגעת פיה לנסיאן אלאמה̈ אללגה̈ וביינת פיה מנאפע אלנט̇אם ואלצ̇מאת וכמא שרחת כ̇תירא מן ד̇לך איצ̇א פי אלי̇ב̇ אלג̇זו אלתי אלפתהא לתצחיח אעראב לגה̈ אלעבראניין פאד̇א קראת אלאמה̈ הד̇א אלכתאב ותעלמה שבאבהא אנתפעת בהד̇ה אלי׳ מנאפע תפצחת פי אללגה̈ ונצ̇אמהא וצמ̇אתהא וכאן פי ד̇לך כ̇ק ישעיהו ולבב נמהרים יבין לדעת ולשון עלגים תמהר לדבר צחות[57]
>
> I likewise explained these three meanings in *The Book of Hebrew Poetry*. It was also in this book that I expressed my grief at the fact that the nation has forgotten the language. In this book I also made clear the benefits of order and connections [of sentences]. I similarly explained many of these ideas also in *The Twelve Parts*, which I composed for correcting the inflection (*iʿrāb*) of the language of the Hebrews. And if the nation reads this book and its youth study it, they will be benefited by these ten benefits: they will become eloquent (*tafaṣṣaḥat*) in the language and its order

[56] For background on *Sefer Ha-Galuy*, see Malter (1913, 487–89; 1921, 269–71) and Harkavy (1891, 133–49).

[57] ≈ وكما شرحت هذه ال-٣ معاني في كتاب الشعر العبراني فتوجعت فيه لنسيان الأمة اللغة وبيّنت فيه منافع النظام والضمات وكما شرحت كثيرا من ذلك أيضا في ال-١٢ الجزء التي ألفتها لتصحيح إعراب لغة العبرانيين فإذا قرأت الأمة هذا الكتاب وتعلمه شبابها انتفعت بهذه ال-١٠ منافع تفصحت في اللغة ونظامها وضماتها وكان في ذلك كقول إشعياء ולבב נמהרים יבין לדעת ולשון עלגים תמהר לדבר צחות.

> and its connection [of sentences], and by that [very thing] will it come about like the saying of Isaiah (32.4), "and the heart of the hasty will understand knowledge and the tongue of the stammerers will hasten to speak clear [things]."

Saadia, making a reference to what he had already expressed in *Sefer Ha-Egron* (*The Book of Hebrew Poetry*), says that he was pained at the fact that the community had forgotten the Hebrew language. Accordingly, he composed both his book on poetry and his work on Hebrew grammar to correct this problem. Interestingly, he expresses his purposes as לתצחיח אעראב לגה̈ אלעבראניין (≈ لتصحيح إعراب لغة العبرانيين) 'for correcting the *iʿrāb* of the language of the Hebrews'. The semantic range of the Arabic term *iʿrāb* is varied. In the Arabic grammatical tradition, it often refers to elements of proper declension or inflection (Lane 1863–1893). Among other Hebrew grammarians writing in Judeo-Arabic, it may refer specifically to the *niqqud* (i.e., vowel pointing; Blau 2006). Given the content of Saadia's grammar book, a similar meaning is also possible here. On the other hand, it could also refer more broadly to correct, clear, or proper language use. Indeed, later in the passage Saadia notes that those who learn from his works will become *faṣīḥ* 'eloquent' in the language.[58] This purpose is then associated with a prophetic verse from Isaiah (32.4), which Saadia quotes in Biblical Hebrew—we will return to the significance of this verse for Saadia's mission and language ideology later. In the meantime, this passage gives rise to a few

---

[58] For a detailed exposition of the term *faṣīḥ* in Saadia, see below.

questions: What was the nature of this *nisyān* ‘forgetting’ of Hebrew? Who exactly was *al-umma* ‘the nation’ who forgot the language? What sort of competence in Hebrew was Saadia hoping to restore to the community? What would be the appropriate venue and context for its use?

A passage from the introduction to *Sefer Ha-Egron* (44–45; Harkavy 1891), the latter part of which we have already treated above (see §1.1.1), may help answer some of these questions (repeated portion from §1.1.1 in grey):

> וכמא ירון בני אסמאעיל אן בעץ̇ כ̇ואצהם ראי קומא לא יפצחון אלכלאם אלערבי פגמה ד̇לך פוצ̇ע להם כלאמא מכ̇תצרא פי כתאב יסתדלון בה עלי אלפציח: כד̇לך ראית כת̇ירא מן בני אסראיל לא יבצרון מרסל פציח לגתנא פכיף עויצה ואד̇א הם תכלמו כאן כת̇ירא ממא ילפט̇ון בה מלחונא ואד̇א הם שערו כאן אלמסתפיץ̇ פי מא בינהם מן אלארכאן אלאואיל הו אלקליל ואלמתרוך הו אכת̇ר: וכד̇לך פי אלקואפי חתי צאר אלכתאב נפסה ענדהם כאלגאמץ̇ מן אלכלאם ואלג̇בי מן אלקול[59]

> And the Ishmaelites also recognise that one of their best saw a people that could not speak the Arabic *kalām* eloquently (*lā yufṣiḥūn*) and this troubled him. So he laid out for them a concise composition in a book, by which they might be guided unto (linguistic) eloquence (*al-faṣīḥ*). In

---

[59] ≈ وكما يرون بني إسماعيل أن بعض خواصهم رأى قوما لا يفصحون الكلام العربي فغمه ذلك فوضع لهم كلاما مختصرا في كتاب يستدلون به على الفصيح. كذلك رأيت كثيرا من بني إسرائيل لا يبصرون مرسل فصيح لغتنا فكيف عويصه وإذا هم تكلموا كان كثيرا مما يلفظون به ملحونا وإذا هم شعروا كان المستفيض في ما بينهم من الأركان الأوائل هو القليل والمتروك هو أكثر. وكذلك في القوافي حتى صار الكتاب نفسه عندهم كالغامض من الكلام والجبى من القول.

> the same way, I have seen many of the Israelites not looking unto that which has been transmitted of the eloquence (*faṣīḥ*) of our language and that which is difficult in it. When they speak, much of what they utter is grammatically wrong. When they compose and recite poetry, that which spreads among them from the ancient foundations (i.e., the poetic rules) is little, and that which is abandoned [so that it is not governed by these rules] is more. And so it is in [their] rhymes, such that the book itself (i.e., the Bible) has become like something obscure to them with respect to [its] idiom or [like] a collection of sayings [without any connection].

The overall hypothesis of our book is that, while it has long been understood that the Hebrew grammatical tradition inherited many of its conventions from the Arabic grammatical tradition, the Hebrew grammarians may also have inherited a language *ideology* from the Arabic grammarians. Although many of the examples adduced in support of our theory require some speculation or inference, this is not at all the case here.

Indeed, this is a key passage to support our overall hypothesis. In this text, Saadia does not reference this Arabic grammarian for the sake of elucidating a point of grammar or comparing morphology. Rather, the reference focuses on the attitude and response of the Arabic grammarian in the face of a linguistic crisis. According to Harkavy (1891, 44–45), בעץ̇ כ̇ואצהם (≈ بعض خواصهم) 'one of their best' may refer to Abū al-ʿAbbās Aḥmad ibn Yaḥyā (d. 904 CE), also known as Thaʿlab. The fact that Saadia compares this Arabic grammarian's situation with his own mission and context is of great interest. Saadia continues by more specifically defining the nature of the linguistic crisis in his own sphere. While he clearly acknowledges the fact that the Jewish community is producing and interacting with Hebrew regularly in different contexts, their competence is inadequate. They have neglected—and thus are not producing—the *mursal* 'that which has been passed down' of the *faṣīḥ* 'eloquence' of the language.

Accordingly, Saadia begins to list a number of ways in which the community is falling short of the *faṣīḥ* of the language. As we have already noted above (see §1.1.1), the contexts in which Saadia critiques the nation's use of language are all performative. Furnishing them with the necessary grammatical material to succeed in these performative areas, then, will become instrumental in helping them on the path to *al-faṣāḥa*, which was a central goal of Saadia's work.

Indeed, as in the Arabic grammarians, the term *faṣāḥa* is especially important in Saadia's language ideology. The precise meaning of this term, however, requires further explication. We may shed further light on how Saadia understood this term (within the context of his own language ideology) by addressing his use of it in the Arabic title of his grammar book.

Though Saadia's Hebrew grammar is commonly referred to as כתב אללגׄה̈ (≈ كتب اللغة) 'The Books of the Language', he also calls it by the name כתאב פציח לגׄה̈ אלעבראניין (≈ كتاب فصيح لغة العبرانيين) 'The Book of the *Faṣīḥ* of the Language of the Hebrews' (Skoss 1952a, 283, 290–91). As hinted at above, much of the significance of this latter title hangs on the interpretation of the word *faṣīḥ*. While Skoss's (1952a, 283, 291) translation of 'elegance' is typical, it may not capture the full sense of what this word would have meant for Saadia. Rather, the precise sense of this word ought to be examined in light of Saadia's other writings and in light of writings from the same period. Such an analysis can even help further clarify Saadia's motivation and purposes in composing 'The Book of the *Faṣīḥ* of the Language of the Hebrews'.

A helpful clue may be found in Dunaš ben Labraṭ's (920–990 CE) references to Saadia's work. Writing in Hebrew, Dunaš does not call Saadia's work by its Arabic title, but rather refers to it in Hebrew by names such as ספר צחות לשון הקדש *sefɛr ṣaḥūṯ lšōn haq-qoḏɛš* 'The Book of the *ṣaḥūṯ* of the Holy Language' and ספר צחות לשון העברי *sefɛr ṣaḥūṯ lšōn hɔ-ʿivrī* 'The Book of the *ṣaḥūṯ* of the Hebrew Language' (Schröter 1866, 26–27; Skoss 1952a, 283; 1952b, 75–76).[60] The word *ṣaḥūṯ* is a noun formed by adding the abstract nominal *-ūṯ* ending to the adjective *ṣaḥ*, which is a particularly rare word in Hebrew, being attested only four times in the entire Bible. In fact, of those four occurrences, it is only used once with reference to language or speaking. This single occurrence is found in Isaiah 32.4.

Fortunately, Saadia's Arabic translation of this verse from Isaiah has been preserved. The Hebrew text of Isaiah 32.4 reads וּלְבַ֣ב נִמְהָרִ֔ים יָבִ֖ין לָדָ֑עַת וּלְשׁ֣וֹן עִלְּגִ֔ים תְּמַהֵ֖ר לְדַבֵּ֥ר צָחֽוֹת׃ 'And the heart of the hasty will understand knowledge, and the tongue of the stammerers will hasten to speak *ṣɔ̄ḥōṯ*'. According to the traditional vocalisation, the Hebrew word *ṣɔ̄ḥōṯ* is the feminine plural form of the adjective *ṣaḥ*. Therefore, the meaning would be something along the lines of 'things that are *ṣaḥ*'. Saadia translates this verse

---

[60] For the vocalisation of consonantal צחות *ṢḤWT* as *ṣaḥūṯ*, see Becker (2013).

into Arabic as וקלוב אלבלדין תפהם אלמערפה̈ ואלסן אלעג̇ם תסרע בכלאם אלפצאחה̈ (≈ وقلوب البلدين تفهم المعرفة وألسن العجم تسرع بكلام الفصاحة) 'and the hearts of the stupid will understand knowledge and the tongues of foreigners will hasten to speak *al-faṣāḥa*' (Derenbourg 1896, 47). What is of particular note here is that Saadia translates the Hebrew word *ṣɔ̄ḥōṯ* as *al-faṣāḥa.*[61] This seems to indicate that Isaiah 32.4 may be connected, at least conceptually, to the title of Saadia's grammar.[62] Further, as we noted at the beginning of this section, Saadia's comments in the introduction to *Sefer Ha-Galuy* understand his grammatical work as a means by which this prophetic verse (Isaiah 32.4) will come to fulfilment. Therefore, it is clear that Saadia was not only aware of this verse from Isaiah, but that it represented the very goal of his work. Accordingly, it would not be over-stepping to suggest that Saadia may have had this verse in mind when he referred to his work as *The Book of the Faṣīḥ of the Language of the Hebrews.*[63]

---

[61] Harkavy calls attention to the relationship between *ṣɔ̄ḥōṯ* and *faṣāḥa* in Saadia's work (Harkavy 1891, 32 n. 3, 32–35, 55 n. 5). He also compares some of Saadia's terminology in the Arabic title of his grammar to parallels among the Arabic grammarians (Harkavy 1891, 32 n. 3).

[62] The connection between *ṣaḥūṯ hal-lɔ̄šōn* 'the *ṣaḥūṯ* of the language', Isaiah 32.4, and Saadia Gaon has already been pointed out in Kokin (2013, 167–68). Kokin highlights the debate about whether there could be any other standard for pure Hebrew than the biblical text itself. According to Kokin, it is in such a context that medieval grammarians were concerned with *ṣaḥūṯ hal-lɔ̄šōn* in the sense of 'purity of language'. For Saadia, the term *ṣaḥūṯ* had a similar connotation regarding conformity with biblical style.

[63] See the previous footnote.

We have thus placed the title of Saadia's grammar within the context of its purpose. We have not yet, however, defined precisely what the content of the words *ṣɔ̄ḥōṯ* or *faṣāḥa* might have been for Saadia.[64] In a roughly contemporary Hebrew-Arabic dictionary, David ben Abraham al-Fāsī (10th c. CE) associates the word *ṣɔ̄ḥōṯ* in Isaiah 32.4 with אלכלאם אלואצ̇ח (≈ الكلام الواضح) 'clear speech' (Skoss 1936–1945, II:505–06). Therefore, in light of Dunaš ben Labraṭ's references to Saadia's title and the fact that Saadia uses the word *faṣāḥa* to translate *ṣɔ̄ḥōṯ*, the title of the book may be better rendered as '*The Book of the Clarity of the Language of the Hebrews*'.[65] It must be stressed, however, that any particular English gloss of *faṣāḥa* or *ṣɔ̄ḥōṯ* in Saadia's works is limited in how much it can convey. The full semantic load carried by these terms can only be clarified by understanding their association with a particular linguistic register of Hebrew.

For this, we may turn to the example of *Sefer Ha-Galuy*. This work was written during Saadia's time in exile after being expelled from the Gaonate by the Exilarch, David ben Zakkai. The main purpose of *Sefer Ha-Galuy* was to vindicate himself in the conflict with David ben Zakkai and defend himself against his detractors. Though the work was first published in Hebrew, it was later supplemented by an Arabic version. It should be noted, however, that the Arabic version was not merely a translation;

---

[64] According to Skoss (1952b, 76), the abstract nominal form *ṣaḥūṯ* refers to 'grammatical correctness of speech', but such a definition raises further questions.

[65] Note also how Malter (1913, 495) translates לְדַבֵּר צָחוֹת *lḏabbēr ṣɔ̄ḥōṯ* as 'to speak plainly'.

rather, it also included a lengthy introduction and explanatory notes of the original Hebrew, and was designed to respond to various accusations that had been made against some of the contents of the earlier Hebrew version (Malter 1921, 269–71). The main part of the book begins as follows (Malter 1921, 389; Harkavy 1891, 180–81):

> דִּבְרֵי סֵפֶר הַגָּלוּי הַכָּמוּס רַאֲוָה וְחָסוּן מוּסָר אִמְרֵי צָחוֹת הֵם אוֹצָרוֹ[66]
>
> The words of *The Open Book*, which is stored-up with observational learning and treasure-laden with moral instruction. The sayings of *ṣɔ̄ḥōṯ* are its treasure (chest).

This short description of the book's contents is telling. It mentions both observational learning and moral instruction as benefits to be derived from it (Malter 1921, 389). The last sentence, however, is curious. In the Arabic note, Saadia explicates אִמְרֵי צָחוֹת *ʾimrē ṣɔ̄ḥōṯ* 'sayings of *ṣɔ̄ḥōṯ*' as אלכלאם אלפציח (≈ الكلام الفصيح) 'eloquent speech' (Harkavy 1891, 181). Moreover, while Malter (1921, 389) understands אוֹצָרוֹ *ʾōṣɔ̄rō* as 'its treasure', both the Hebrew term and its explication in the Arabic note as כ̇זנה (≈ خزنه) may point more towards the idea of a 'storehouse'.[67] Therefore, while we should not disregard the fact that Saadia regards the sayings of *ṣɔ̄ḥōṯ* as a sort of treasure in themselves, he may be

---

[66] *divrē sefɛr hag-gɔ̄lūy hak-kɔ̄mūs raʾavɔ̄ v-ḥɔ̄sūn mūsɔ̄r ʾimrē ṣāḥōṯ hēm ʾōṣɔ̄rō.*

[67] See also Saadia's translation of אוֹצְרֹתָי *ʾōṣrōṯɔ̄y* as כ̇זאיני (≈ خزائني) 'my vaults; my treasuries' in Deut. 32.34 as support for the translation of 'storehouse'. For Saadia's translation of Deut. 32.34, see Bodenheimer (1856, 67).

saying that they are actually a kind of storehouse—or treasure 'chest'—in which the learning and moral instruction is brought to the reader. That is, the 'sayings of *ṣɔ̄ḥōṯ*' would not merely be referring to a particular section or an occasional proverb found in the book, but rather to the style of language used consistently throughout the entirety of the work. The linguistic style itself is the means by which the learning and moral instruction is communicated. On this point, it is worth noting that the moralistic dimension of proper or correct speech is part of the concept of a standard language ideology. Utilising a special cultural possession (i.e., the standard language) for performance in the public sphere should require professional capabilities, including moral authority. Linguistic competence and morality thus go hand-in-hand in this case.

What, then, is the type of language used by Saadia in *Sefer Ha-Galuy*? Beyond any doubt, it is marked by a relentless attempt to imitate and reproduce the Hebrew characteristic of the Bible (Malter 1913, 488; Malter 1921, 269).[68] In the mind of Saadia, then, the words *ṣɔ̄ḥōṯ* and *al-faṣāḥa* were to be applied primarily to the Hebrew language and style characteristic of the Bible.[69] Moreover, Saadia notes that he wrote the book עבר[א]ניא מפסקא פואסיקא מסמנא מטעמא (≈ عبرانيا مفسقا فواسيفا مسمنا مطعما) 'in Hebrew, versed with verses, pointed (with vowels), and accented (with

[68] See the beginning of the main Hebrew section in Harkavy (1891, 180–81); Schechter (1903, 4–7).

[69] In *Sefer Ha-Egron* (his book on Hebrew poetry), however, Saadia does not have a problem with citing extra-biblical 'ancient' poets as examples of good Hebrew poetry (see chapter 4, §2.1.3).

ṭeʿamim)' (Malter 1913, 490, 496). In other words, Saadia did not only imitate the biblical style of language, but he formatted his book exactly like the biblical text (Malter 1913, 488; Malter 1921, 269). This sort of orthographic and codicological presentation thus serves to guide the process of enregisterment (see chapter 3, §2.2) with respect to Saadia's own compositions as exemplary models of pure and correct Hebrew. In other words, the 'biblical' traits of the physical artefact of the text itself would thus encourage readers to enregister the linguistic signs used by Saadia to an idealised 'biblical' register. In sum, it is the style of Hebrew exemplified in Saadia's poetic compositions in *Sefer Ha-Galuy* that is to serve as an exemplar for the nation to imitate in its quest to achieve Hebrew eloquence.

That Saadia regarded his poetic Hebrew compositions in *Sefer Ha-Galuy* in this way is further confirmed by another passage from the book, in which he outlines his plans to restore *al-faṣāḥa* to the people (Malter 1913, 493–94, 498–99; Harkavy 1891, 156–57):

> ואלת̇אני תעלים אלאמה̈ תאליף̇ אלכלאם וגבסה אד̇ געלת הד̇א כאלסראג̇ יחד̇ון חד̇וה ויתנבהון בה עלי נט̇אם כ̇טאבהם ומעאניהם: ואלת̇אלת̇ תעלימהא אלצ̇מאת אד̇ כאן כל כלאם לא תכמל מערפתה אלא בצ̇מאת מגמעה̈ פי אלקול בעצ̇ אלי בעצ̇ חתי תצח̈ בד̇לך אלמעאני ואלא פסדת ותגיירת[70]
>
> The second [part] is teaching the nation how to compose *kalām* and its obscurity. Therefore, I have made this [book]

---

[70] ≈ والثاني تعليم الأمة تأليف الكلام وغبسه إذ جعلت هذا كالسراج يحذون حذوه ويتنبهون به على نظام خطابهم ومعانيهم. والثالث تعليمها الضمات إذ كان كل كلام لا تكمل معرفته إلا بضمات مجمعة في القول بعض إلى بعض حتى تصحّ بذلك المعاني وإلا فسدت وتغيّرت.

> as a lamp, the example of which they should imitate (*yaḥḏūn ḥaḏwahu*), and by which they should have brought to their attention [the proper] ordering of their discourse and meanings. The third [part] is teaching them the connections [of sentences], since the sense of every speech (*kalām*) would not be complete, except by connections [of sentences] that are combined with one another in the saying so that the meanings become clear by that [very thing]. Otherwise, it is corrupted and changed.

It is clear from the first passage of *Sefer Ha-Galuy* examined in this section that Saadia hoped to help the nation become *faṣīḥ* through reading and studying his grammar book. This passage, however, confirms what we have just now argued about his less explicit (and complementary) method of instructing the community. He says that he has made the book כאלסראג̇ יחד̇ון חד̇וה (≈ كالسراج يحذون حذوه) 'as a lamp, the example of which they should imitate'. The community can become *faṣīḥ* not only by learning grammar in a systematic way through *Kitāb faṣīḥ lughat al-ʿibrāniyyīn*, but also by imitating the Hebrew style of Saadia himself in *Sefer Ha-Galuy*.[71] This, of course, is consistent with the fact that Saadia wrote the entire book in biblical style.

Whether writing a grammar book containing systematic instruction in Biblical Hebrew (e.g., *Kitāb faṣīḥ lughat al-ʿibrāniyyīn*) or composing poetry as a literary exemplar to be imitated (e.g., *Sefer Ha-Galuy*), then, Saadia frames his work as a response to נסיאן אלאמה̈ אללגה̈ (≈ نسيان الأمة اللغة) 'the nation forgetting the language'. From an ideological perspective, all such work of Saadia

---

[71] According to Malter (1921, 269), one purpose of *Sefer Ha-Galuy* was that "it serve as a model of elegant Hebrew style."

was motivated by the disappointment he experienced at seeing just how much the *faṣīḥ* of the language (i.e., biblical style) had been neglected among the nation. This 'complaint tradition' (see chapter 3, §§2.1.4–2.1.5) thus became the catalyst for his mission to restore *al-faṣāḥa* to the nation through his grammar book and other writings.

2.1.2. Judah ben David Ḥayyūj (945–1000 CE)

While we have treated the theme of a 'complaint tradition' in Saadia's works most extensively, we also find evidence of this same phenomenon among other Hebrew grammarians. The passage from the introduction to Ḥayyūj's (945–1000 CE) work on weak verbal morphology—though already treated above in part (see §1.1.2) due to its relevance for the performance contexts of Hebrew usage—is also relevant here. We thus address it now in its fuller context, breaking it into parts (*Kitāb al-afʿāl ḏawāt ḥurūf al-līn*, 1; Jastrow 1897):

> قال يحيى بن داود غَرَضِى فى هذا الكتاب الإبانةُ عن حروف اللين والمدّ العبرانيّة التنبيهُ على أنحائها وتصاريفِها فقد خَفِىَ امرُها عن كثير من الناس للينها واعتلالها ودقّة معانيها وبُعد غورها فلا يدرون كيف تتصرّف الافعال ذوات حُرُوف اللين وكثيرا ما يستعملونها فى خُطَبِهِمْ واشعارهم على غَيْرِ ٱلصّواب
>
> Yaḥyā ibn Dāwūd (i.e., Ḥayyūj) said, "My purpose (*gharaḍī*) in [writing] this book is to clarify the Hebrew weak and elongated letters (i.e., semivowels) and to call attention to their various forms and conjugations. The matter of [the conjugation of weak verbs] has been hidden from many of the people with respect to their weakness, defectiveness,

precise meanings, and the extent of their declivity, so that they do not know how weak verbs conjugate and they frequently use them (*yastaʿmilūnahā*) in their speeches (*fī ḫuṭabihim*) and their poems (*ašʿārihim*) in an incorrect manner (*ʿalā ghayr al-ṣawāb*)."

Ḥayyūj begins this section by explicitly stating that his purpose in writing his book was to clarify weak verbal morphology in response to the fact that people regularly misconjugate weak verbs in their speeches and poems. As was the case with Saadia, the impetus for writing a grammatical work was witnessing the corruption or neglect of pure and correct Hebrew among the masses. The grammatical treatise is thus meant to help the people recover the *faṣāḥa* of Hebrew, namely that which is consistent with biblical style and norms. He then goes on to cite some examples of such misconjugations in roughly contemporary compositions (*Kitāb al-afʿāl ḏawāt ḥurūf al-līn*, 1–2; Jastrow 1897):

ويسلكون بها غَيْرَ سبيل الحَقّ كمن قال فى بعض كلامه הן נמצא האדם
נודע טרם הבראו ומקודש טרם צְרוֹתוֹ اشتقّ צְרוֹתוֹ بزعمه من יָצַר יָצַרְתִּי
ولم يَشْعُرْ بانّ مثل هذا المصدر لا يكون إلا من الافعال التى لامُها حرف لين
كما سنبيّن وقال ايضا מה לבני פרחח לָעוּד בנזם וחח أَخَذَ לָעוּד بظنّه من
וְעָדִית עֶדִי תַּעְדֶּה כליה עֲדֵה־נא גאון וגבה ولم يأْبه انّ مثله لا يكون إلّا من
فعل عينُه حرف لين كما سيتّضح ذلك مما أَسْتَأْنِفُ شَرْحَهُ

And they use [weak verbs] in an improper way, like someone who said in one of his sayings (*kalām*), "Behold, the man was found—known—before he was created, and sanctified before he was formed (*ṣrōṯō*)," in which he derived 'his forming (*ṣrōṯō*)' by asserting that it was (the infinitive) of 'he formed (*yɔ̄ṣar*), I formed (*yɔ̄ṣartī*)', yet was not aware that such an infinitive does not inflect as if it were from a

> root whose third consonant is weak, as we will clarify [later]. [The same one] also said, "Why should the children of the buds adorn themselves (*lɔʿūḏ*) with brooches and earrings?" taking 'to adorn (*lɔʿūḏ*)' as if it is from "and you shall adorn yourself with an ornament (*v-ʿɔḏīṯ ʿɛḏī*)" (Ezek. 23.40), "she shall put on (*taʿdɛ*) her ornaments" (Isa. 61.10), and "adorn yourself (*ʿaḏē*) with majesty and exaltation!" (Job 40.10). But he was not sensitive to the fact that such verbs are not based on roots with a weak second radical, as will become clear from my upcoming exposition of the topic.

In the first example, Ḥayyūj criticises the form צְרוֹתוֹ *ṣrōṯō* 'his forming' as an improper formation of the infinitive of יָצַר *yɔṣar* as if it were a III-y root instead of a I-y root. Presumably, though unattested in the Bible, the proper infinitive would be something like יְצֹר *yṣōr*. In the second example, Ḥayyūj critiques the form לָעוּד *lɔʿūḏ* as an improper formation of the infinitive of עָדָה *ʿɔḏɔ* as if it were a II-w root instead of a III-y root. Presumably, though also absent from the Bible, the 'correct' form would be something like לַעֲדוֹת *laʿaḏōṯ*. Both examples identified as mistakes by Ḥayyūj are from the *Maḥberet* of the tenth-century Andalusian philologist and poet Menaḥem ben Saruq (ca 920–ca 970 CE), who also happened to be Ḥayyūj's teacher (Yahalom and Katsumata 2014, 104). Without quoting any authors specifically, Ḥayyūj then goes on to cite many examples of misconjugation of weak roots.

It is significant to note, however, that such examples based on analogy actually have a long history in Hebrew, even within the Bible itself. Note how an analogy comparable to יְצֹר *yṣōr* → צְרוֹת *ṣrōṯ* is also found in the biblical example סְפוֹת *sfōṯ* (from the root *y-s-p*) 'adding' (Isa. 30.1). Similarly, an analogy comparable to עֲדוֹת *ʿaḏōṯ* → עוּד *ʿūḏ* is attested in the biblical form לָבְוּז: *lɔ̄vūz* (from the root *b-z-y*) 'to be despised' (Prov. 12.8). In light of such comparable analogies, Ḥayyūj's insistence that the forms used by Menaḥem ben Saruq are 'incorrect' reflects the codification of a 'standard' language with more regularity even than the Bible itself, even though what is 'correct' is presented as that which is consistent with the Bible. Moreover, it also ignores the fact that such forms could develop naturally or even artfully in a living and dynamic performance language, just as many comparable analogies occur in the *piyyuṭim* (Rand 2014, 158–59). Ḥayyūj may thus be correcting linguistic norms that developed naturally in a performance context and attempting to bring them more into conformity with a general systematised and regularised paradigm of 'Biblical Hebrew' morphology.

Ḥayyūj goes on to lament the state of the language if such misconjugations are allowed. When the speaker can conjugate weak verbs كيف ما اراد 'however he wants'—presumably with some analogical basis—then the following occurs (*Kitāb al-afʿāl ḏawāt ḥurūf al-līn*, 2–3; Jastrow 1897):

> فتنهدم حينئذ أبنية اللغة وَتُخْرَبُ حدودُها وتنهدّ اسوارها لِأنّ الفعل الذى فاؤه حرف لين يرجِع فعلا عينه او لامه حرف لين وكذلك... ولمّا رايت هذا التغيير الواقع فى حروف اللين خاصّة وضعت فيها بتأييد الله وعونه هذا الكتاب الذى بيّنت فيه انحائَها وتصاريفها
>
> The structures of the language are thus demolished, its borders are laid waste, and its walls are collapsed, since a verb whose first root consonant is weak becomes a verb whose

> second or third root consonant is weak, etc.... When I observed such interchanges happening particularly with the weak consonants, I composed this book about it—with the help and support of God—in which I clarified their various forms and conjugations.

As the passage continues, Ḥayyūj waxes poetic in his description of just how much destruction has befallen the language as a result of such a cavalier treatment of weak verbs among orators and poets. This constitutes an example of the 'complaint tradition' *par excellence*. And, once again, in response to the corruption of the language by the masses, Ḥayyūj decides to compose this book to clarify the proper conjugation of such forms. As already noted above, however, Ḥayyūj 'clarifying' the correct conjugation of such forms is actually Ḥayyūj himself attempting to institutionalise what he believes *should be* the 'standard' form of the language based on his own language ideology of what constitutes pure Hebrew.

He goes on to explain his methods in determining what constitutes a proper form to include in the book. By gathering all attested weak verbal forms in the Bible, he is able either to establish a 'correct' form based on attestation or to reconstruct it based on *qiyās* 'systematic analogy' to attested forms. The result of this scouring and extension of biblical data Ḥayyūj explains as follows (*Kitāb al-afʿāl ḏawāt ḥurūf al-līn*, 3; Jastrow 1897):

> ليكون ذلك أَتَمَّ فى ما قصدت بيانه وأَبْلَغَ فى ما نويت من الانتفاع بالكتاب إنْ شاء الله وما حضرنى فى حكاية ذلك ووصفِه شىء من اللفظ الجيّد الفصيح ونظام الكلام ٱلْمُتْقَنِ

> ...so that this will be the most comprehensive [version] of what I set out to clarify and the most eloquent (*ablagh*) of what I intended in terms of deriving benefit from the book (*al-kitāb*), if God wills it. And what has prepared me to make an account and description of this is something of good eloquent (*faṣīḥ*) diction and perfect order of speech (*kalām*)...

According to Ḥayyūj, his book will comprehensively provide the reader with everything necessary to use weak verbs correctly and eloquently. As the passage continues, he goes on to describe the result of giving heed to his work, namely replicating the eloquence of the 'ancient Hebrews', which passage we have already quoted and discussed earlier in this volume (see chapter 4, §2.1.1). It should also be noted that Ḥayyūj feels the need to establish his own credentials. He is equipped to determine the correct forms of weak verbs because he himself has already achieved something of eloquence with respect to correct Hebrew. By first critiquing the Hebrew of others and subsequently setting himself up as an authority fit to determine proper forms, he both furthers the complaint tradition and (implicitly) encourages his readers to enregister the form of Hebrew he is codifying as *faṣīḥ*.

2.1.3. David ben Abraham al-Fāsī (10th c. CE)

David ben Abraham al-Fāsī (10th c. CE) also seems to view the composition of his lexicon against the backdrop of the deterioration of Hebrew among the masses. When discussing his methods and motivations for writing his lexicon, he writes the following (Skoss 1936–1945, I:1):

פראית אסיר סירה̈ מן תקדמני פי ד̇לך ואקצד קצדהם ומאכ̇ד̇הם כ̇אצה̈
פי מעני אלתרתיב ואלנסק ואן כ̇אלפת אלעבארה̈ פי בעץ̇ מא חכוה פלא
צ̇ר̈ אד̇ לם תזאל אלעלמא מכ̇תלפין מן חית̇ קד פאתתנא לגתנא ונחן גיר
מסתעמלין אלפאט̇הא פאנדרסת חיניד̇ ובעדת אגראצ̇הא ואסתגרקת
מעאניהא[72]

I saw fit to follow in the footsteps of those who have gone before me in this and to pursue their purpose and method, especially with respect to the meaning of arrangement and order. And if the expression differs among some of those who have reported it, then [it must be said] that there is no harm if scholars remain divided with respect to how our language has come down to us, especially when we ourselves are unable to use its words, since otherwise it would be wiped out (*indarasat*), its usages would become remote (*baʿudat*), and its meanings would be buried (*istaghraqat*).

Al-Fāsī appears to exhibit somewhat more humility in his attitude towards the language and its grammar than Saadia or Ḥayyūj. He acknowledges, first of all, that he is following in the footsteps of previous grammarians and lexicographers. There are thus cases where various scholars exhibit disagreement with respect to a particular Hebrew word. Nevertheless, rather than abandon the work or set himself up as the sole authority on a particular matter, he allows for variance of opinion—a common

---

72 ≈ فرأيت أسير سيرة من تقدمني في ذلك وأقصد قصدهم ومأخذهم خاصة في معنى الترتيب والنسق وإن خالفت العبارة في بعض ما حكوه فلا ضرّ إذ لم تزال العلماء مختلفين من حيث قد فاتتنا لغتنا ونحن غير مستعملين ألفاظها فاندرست حينئذ وبعدت أغراضها واستغرقت معانيها.

feature of Karaite thought during this period—since the most important thing is to provide resources for keeping knowledge of Hebrew alive in the community.

What al-Fāsī is essentially saying here is that even though there may not be a consensus among scholars regarding certain words, the need to restore proper Hebrew is so dire—the people (including himself) are not really using the language at this point—that it is far more important to address the urgent need and to supply the people with some kind of guidance than to have the language be lost. Without at least making some attempt to restore Hebrew proficiency, the language would be wiped out (אנדרסת ≈ اندرست), its usages would become remote (בעדת ≈ بعدت), and its meanings would be buried (אסתגרקת ≈ استغرقت).

On this point, it is significant that he does not 'other' the community who has neglected the language in the way that Saadia and Ḥayyūj do. Rather, he includes himself in those neglecting the language by noting that scholarly caution is irrelevant and unnecessary ונחן גיר מסתעמלין אלפאט̇הא (≈ ونحن غير مستعملين ألفاظها) 'while *we ourselves* are unable to use its words'. Indeed, as Milroy points out, the 'complaint tradition' is not limited to those whose voices are considered authoritative on language. It is also often found among language users who regard themselves as part of the community neglecting the language (see chapter 3, §§2.1.4–2.1.5). This likely shows just how far such an ideology has penetrated into the community, which serves to further solidify the canonicity of the 'standard' language outside of everyday speech and colloquial language.

Al-Fāsī's more modest posture towards his own linguistic proficiency can also be seen in his apologetic for his authorship of his lexicon (Skoss 1936–1945, I:1–2):

> פנבתדי במא אועדנא בה מן תאליף הד̇א אלכתאב וד̇כר כל מא תצ̇מנתה
> מעאניה ואחו́תה אבואבה מן לגה̈ אלעבראניה̈ ושרח גואמצ̇הא ואיצ̇אח
> גפלאתהא חסב אלטאקה̈ ואלג̇הד מע מא אני ענד רוחי אקל מחל [פי
> אלרפ]קה̈ ואנזל דרג̇ה̈ מן אן אתקדם עלי תרג̇מה̈ אללגה̈ ואן̈ תקדמי עלי
> ד̇לך פממא דעת אלצ̇רורה̈ אלי מת̇לי לא ען קוה̈ אג̇דהא פוק אהל זמאני
> בל מעתרף אנא בנקצי ומ́קר̈ בצ̇עף עלמי ואני לאחוג̇ אלי אלתעלים מן אן
> אעלם גירי ולכן מן וג̇ה אלסיאסה̈ אן ירסם אל[קא]ר חסב מא קד עלמה
> ליכון מוג̇ודא ללקאצד אלנט̇ר פיה[73]
>
> We shall begin with what we have promised with respect to composing this book, mentioning whatever of its meanings and chapters comprise it with respect to the Hebrew language, interpreting its riddles, and clarifying its neglected areas according to the energy and effort [that lie within me]. [And this I will do], even though I strongly feel that I deserve the lowest place among the company (of grammarians, lexicographers, etc.) and am of too low of a rank to be worthy of taking up the task of interpreting and explaining the language. That someone like me should even take up this task is merely due to the fact that necessity (*al ḍarūra*) requires it; it is not at all due to any

---

73 ≈ فنبتدئ بما أوعدنا به من تأليف هذا الكتاب وذكر كل ما تضمنته معانيه وأحوَته أبوابه من لغة العبرانية وشرح غوامضها وإيضاح غفلاتها حسب الطاقة والجهد مع ما أني عند روحي أقل محل في الرفقة وأنزل درجة من أن أتقدم على ترجمة اللغة وأنّ تقدمي على ذلك فمما دعت الضرورة إلى مثلي لا عن قوة أجدها فوق أهل زماني بل معترف أنا بنقصي ومُقرّ بضعف علمي وأني لأحوَج إلى التعليم من أن أعلّم غيري ولكن من وجه السياسة أن يرسم القارئ(؟) حسب ما قد علمه ليكون موجودا للقاصد النظر فيه.

> strength I find in myself above my contemporaries (*ahl zamānī*). Rather, I readily acknowledge my own lack and accept the weakness of my own knowledge and that I am in greater need of instruction than of teaching someone else. Nevertheless, for reasons of expediency, the reader/writer/artist(?) should sketch according to what he already knows so that it will be present for the one who wants to look at it.

Even though this passage is clearly written within the framework of a 'complaint tradition', its tone starkly contrasts with that of Saadia and Ḥayyūj. Al-Fāsī is careful to point out to his readers that even he is not among the most exemplary of language users. Ironically, however, it is this modesty that more prominently reinforces the standard language ideology and the conviction that the canonical form of the language has been neglected among the masses. If even a prominent lexicographer like al-Fāsī does not know the language sufficiently, then surely the state of Hebrew knowledge among the community is in dire straits. The fact that al-Fāsī, unworthy in his own eyes, nevertheless endeavours to compose his lexicon underscores just how powerfully the need was felt. The way in which he frames this need, in turn, serves to elevate the value of Hebrew proficiency among the community.

2.2. Comparison with the Arabic Tradition

The idea that pure and correct language had been neglected or corrupted among the masses, as comports with the 'complaint tradition', is also quite prevalent among the Arabic grammarians. Moreover, as Brustad (2016, 154) has demonstrated, from an ideological perspective, some of the Arabic grammarians frame the emergence of grammar as a response to this deterioration of the language among the masses.

2.2.1. Ibn Sallām al-Jumaḥī (d. 845/846 CE)

Ibn Sallām al-Jumaḥī (d. 845/846 CE), for example, when discussing the history of the Arabic language and the Baṣran grammarians in his book about poets (*Ṭabaqāt fuḥūl al-šuʿarāʾ*; Ibrāhīm 2001, 1.29), writes the following about Abū al-Aswad al-Duʾalī (d. 688/689 CE):[74]

> وكان لأهل البصرة في العربيّة قدْمة بالنَّحْو وبلُغات العرب والغريب عناية وكان أوّلَ من أسّس العربيّة وفتَح بابَها وأَنْهَج سبيلها ووضع قياسها أبو الأَسْوَدِ الدُؤَليُّ وهو ظالم بن عمرو بن سفيان بن جندل وكان رجل أهل البصرة وكان علوِيَّ الرّأيْ... وإنّما قال ذاك حين اضطرب كلامُ العرب فغلبتْ السليقية فكان سراةُ الناس يَلْحَنون فوضع بابَ الفاعلِ والمفعولِ والمضافِ وحروفِ الجرّ والرَّفْعِ والنَّصْبِ والجَزْمِ
>
> The Baṣrans have chronological preeminence in the *ʿarabiyya* with respect to grammar (*naḥw*), the dialects of the Arabs (*lughāt al-ʿarab*), and less-attended-to rare forms (*al-gharīb ʿināyat-an*). The first one who founded (*assasa*) the *ʿarabiyya*, pioneered its treatment as a subject (*fataḥa bābaha*), traced its path (*anhaja sabīlahā*), and codified its rules (*waḍaʿa qiyāsahā*) was Abū al-Aswad al-Duʾalī, that is Ẓālim ibn ʿAmr ibn Sufyān ibn Jandal. Now he was a Baṣran man of superior intelligence.... [Al-Duʾalī did all

[74] Portions of this passage are mentioned in Brustad (2016, 154).

> this][75] when the speech of the Arabs (*kalām al-ʿarab*) became disturbed (*iḍṭaraba*) and native speech (*al-salīqiyya*) took over. The leaders of the people were committing grammatical errors, so he composed a chapter on the 'agent' (*al-fāʿil*), the 'patient' (*al-mafʿūl*), the bound form in an *iḍāfa* construction (*al-muḍāf*), prepositions (*ḥurūf al-jarr*), the nominative (*al-rafʿ*), the accusative (*al-naṣb*), and the shortened prefix conjugation (*al-jazm*).

In this passage, Ibn Sallām credits Abū al-Aswad al-Duʾalī (d. 688/689 CE) with founding the Arabic grammatical tradition, at least with respect to its written codification. What is most significant from an ideological perspective, however, is that the "emergence of grammar" came about when اضطرب كلام العرب 'the speech of the Arabs became disturbed' (Brustad 2016, 154). As a result of this disturbance in the transmission of the *ʿarabiyya*—quite plausibly the elevated performance register of the Arabic language—and its corpus, غلبت السليقية 'native speech took over'.[76]

---

[75] Lit.: 'And this he said...'. Although the syntax is odd here, it is more clear in the formulation of al-Zubaydī (d. 989 CE) in his *Ṭabaqāt al-naḥwiyyīn wa-l-lughawiyyīn* (Ibrāhīm 1973, 21): وهو أول من أسس العربية، ونهج سبُلَها، ووضع قياسها؛ وذلك حين اضطرب كلام العرب 'and [al-Duʾalī] was the first who founded the *ʿarabiyya*, traced its paths, and codified its rules, and this when *kalām al-ʿarab* became disturbed'.

[76] Further support for the idea that the *ʿarabiyya* and its corpus had to be transmitted faithfully is found in a passage in al-Fārābī (d. 950 CE) in which he discusses الذين نقلوا اللغة 'those who transmitted the language' and الذي نقل اللغة واللسان العربي 'those who transmitted the language, that is the Arabic language' (see §3.2.2).

The term *salīqiyya* has a number of nuances with respect to speech. Its connotations include not only that which is natural dialectally but also that which is free from elements acquired through learning, perhaps such as certain aspects of *iʿrāb* (Lane 1863–1893). This brought about a situation in which كان سراة الناس يلحنون 'the leaders of the people were committing grammatical errors' (Brustad 2016, 154). Consistent with the 'complaint tradition', then, the initial codification of grammar is ideologically framed as a response to the prevalence of linguistic errors among the masses. It is worth noting, however, that the disturbance of *kalām al-ʿarab* is blamed specifically on the people's preoccupation with the wars of conquest later in Ibn Sallām's work (Ibrāhīm 2001, 1.34; Brustad 2016, 154).

2.2.2. al-Jāḥiẓ (d. 868/869 CE)

The complaint tradition is also quite clearly exemplified in al-Jāḥiẓ's (d. 868/869 CE) *Al-bayān wa-l-tabyīn*. After recounting the fact that some have gotten used to خطأ 'error' and كلام العلوج 'coarse speech' in Arabic, he writes the following (1.162; Haroun 1998):

> فمن زعم أنَّ البلاغةَ أن يكون السامعُ يفهمُ معنى القائلِ، جعل الفصاحةَ واللُّكنة، والخطأَ والصَّوابَ، والإغلاق والإبانة، والملحونَ والمُعْرب، كله سواءً، وكلّه بياناً
>
> So he who claims that eloquence (*al-balāgha*) is [merely] about the hearer being able to understand the meaning of the speaker has thus regarded eloquence (*al-faṣāḥa*) as equivalent to improper speech (*al-lukna*), error (*al-ḫaṭaʾ*)

> as equivalent to correctness (*al-ṣawāb*), obscurity as equivalent to clarity, ungrammaticality (*al-malḥūn*) as equivalent to proper speech (*al-muʿrab*), and all of it alike as elegant expression (*bayān*).

This comment occurs within the context of a longer passage in which al-Jāḥiẓ cites a number of grammatical errors made by the people. This particular instantiation of the complaint tradition is also part of a larger discourse in al-Jāḥiẓ that endeavours to elevate the Arabic spoken in Arabia, and especially that of the period of Muhammad. However, despite his complaints about the error-ridden speech of the people, because al-Jāḥiẓ presents the locus of pure Arabic among the Bedouin of the desert, especially those of the past, his readers are left without any direct access to those who could improve their ineloquence. As a result, they have to trust al-Jāḥiẓ to instruct them, since he has put in the work to acquire competence in proper Arabic speech (Webb 2016, 299–301). Naturally, this ties into the 'fieldwork *topos*' examined earlier (see chapter 4, §3.2.3).

2.2.3. *Laḥn al-ʿāmma* Genre

Also relevant here as a particular instantiation of the complaint tradition is the genre known as *laḥn al-ʿāmma* 'solecisms (i.e., grammatical errors) of the lower classes', which came about as standard language ideology became more embedded in the culture. In fact, Brustad (2017, 50) argues that the complaint tradition had become so entrenched in Arabic that it may be regarded as a 'complaint genre'.

The *laḥn al-ʿāmma* genre generally consists of an opposition between what *al-ʿāmma* say as opposed to what *should* be said, with the former often being introduced by phrases like تقول ‘you say…’ or يقولون ‘they say…’ and the latter being introduced by phrases like والصواب ‘whereas the norm/correct form is…’. In other cases, the correct form is introduced by تقول ‘you *shall* say…’, whereas the incorrect form is introduced by لا تقول ‘you *shall not* say…’ (Pellat 2012). In still other cases, the incorrect form might also be introduced by لا يقال ‘*shall not* be said…’.

Note the following example contrasting two ways of expressing the patient of an action—prepositional phrases vs object suffixes on a verb—in the work *Kitāb mā talḥan fīhi al-ʿāmma/al-ʿawāmm* (Abdel-Tawāb 1982, 102–03), attributed to al-Kisāʾī (d. 804/805 CE), though some dispute this attribution (see Pellat 2012):

> وتقول: شكرتُ لك، ونصحتُ لك. ولا يقال: شكرتُك ونصحتُك. وقد نصح فلان لفلان، وشكر له. هذا كلام العرب. قال الله تعالى: «اشْكُرْ لِي وَلِوَالِدَيْكَ»
>
> You shall say, ‘I thanked you (*šakartu laka*)’ and ‘I counselled you (*naṣaḥtu laka*)’, but [the following] shall not be said: ‘I thanked you (*šakartuka*)’ or ‘I counselled you (*naṣaḥtuka*)’. And ‘so-and-so counselled so-and-so (*naṣaha li-fulān*)’ and ‘thanked him (*šakara lahu*)’. This is *kalām al-ʿarab*. God the Exalted One said, “Be thankful to mc (*uškur lī*) and to your parents” (Luqman [31.14]).

Presumably, those portions introduced by لا يقال ‘*shall not* be said…’ are based on expressions current among the speech of *al-ʿāmma/al-ʿawāmm*, whoever they might have been, whereas those portions introduced by تقول ‘you *shall* say…’ reflect the prescriptions of the grammarians, which are described as being consistent with *kalām al-ʿarab*. As a whole, then, the *laḥn al-ʿāmma* genre points to a belief that the proper form of the language has been neglected among the masses, who thus require instruction from linguistic authorities to recover it.

It may be that the *laḥn al-ʿāmma* genre was meant to help speakers correct the sorts of mistakes that they would make in oral performances. This may be indicated by the categories of *laḥn* treated by Ibn al-Sikkīt (d. 857/858 CE) in his *Iṣlāḥ al-manṭiq* 'Benefitting Pronunciation', where he treats semantic oppositions between homographic patterns like *faʿl* vs *fiʿl* (= فعل), *fiʿl* vs *fuʿl* (= فعل), etc. These are the sorts of errors one might make if they only learned such words through reading or if there was regional variation in the nominal patterns of such words (Brustad 2010).

2.3. Analysis

In both the Hebrew and Arabic grammatical traditions, the composition of grammatical works—or its initial emergence as a discipline—is ideologically cast as a response to the deterioration of proper language use among the masses. In particular, witnessing grammatical mistakes by those engaging in the (performance) language—or complete neglect of it—is often what motivates the grammarian to compose his grammatical work. Ḥayyūj, for example, states that those delivering speeches and composing poetry misconjugate weak verbs. Saadia laments the nation's *nisyān* 'forgetting' of the language. Al-Fāsī acknowledges that proper Hebrew has been neglected to such an extent that the community (including himself) no longer even uses its words. He himself falls short of linguistic proficiency. In the Arabic tradition, this is paralleled by Ibn Sallām's report that *kalām al-ʿarab* became disturbed and neglected during the Islamic conquests. As a result, even the leaders of the people were making grammatical mistakes. We might also note that the nature and content of Ḥayyūj's treatise, namely pointing out morphological 'errors' and providing the 'correct' forms, is reminiscent of the sorts of لا تقول 'you *shall not* say…' vs تقول 'you *shall* say…' oppositions found in the *laḥn al-ʿāmma* genre of the Arabic tradition. The identification of speech errors is also found in al-Jāḥiẓ's *Al-bayān wa-l-tabyīn*.

In all of these cases, then, it becomes the hope of the grammarian that providing the people with grammatical resources will encourage a 'return' to linguistic proficiency in the pure language. In both Saadia and Ḥayyūj, it is believed that attending to their works will lead their readers to become *faṣīḥ* in the language like their biblical ancestors. Al-Fāsī, more modestly, is just trying to prevent the language from being wiped out entirely. Abū al-Aswad al-Duʾalī very practically begins with an exposition of various grammatical features (e.g., 'agent', 'patient', case system), presumably to encourage proper usage.

These trends in both traditions continue multiple themes of a standard language ideology, especially that of the 'complaint tradition' (see chapter 3, §§2.1.4–2.1.5). Critiquing the community for linguistic mistakes also upholds the belief that there are 'correct' and 'incorrect' forms of the language apart from any reference to mutual intelligibility or functionality (see chapter 3, §2.1.3). This is especially clear in Ḥayyūj's critique of 'misconjugating' weak verbs in speeches and poems. Moreover, the fact that grief at the community's linguistic failures is often expressed in relation to their 'forgetting' or 'losing' the language, which was better known in earlier times, also serves to underscore the idea that the language is a cultural possession (see chapter 3, §2.1.1), even if the people have not treated it with the value it deserves. Finally, that the complaint tradition served as the catalyst for the composition of grammatical treatises also feeds into other elements of a standard language ideology. In particular, composing a grammar institutionalises and/or serves to maintain the standard canonical language (see chapter 3, §2.1.6). Depending on how the work of grammar is presented in relation to various cultural values—especially with respect to its author and its codicological format—it may also encourage readers to enregister the linguistic features described therein to a particular variety or register (chapter 3, §2.2).

3.0. Blaming Foreign Languages: تَنَبَّطَتْ قراءتهم

With all the 'complaining' of the grammarians about the linguistic deficiencies of the masses—and how they 'forgot' the language—one of their contemporaries might wonder why this happened in the first place. If this was not always the case, what caused the Hebrew linguistic abilities of the masses to decline so precipitously? At least at some point in the history of both grammatical traditions, the influx of foreigners and/or foreign languages are blamed for the decline of proficiency in the standard language among the people. What is particularly interesting in each tradition, however, is how grammarians of different times and/or cultural contexts hold different views on this matter. In some cases, certain societal changes that took place over time might have given rise to such a negative attitude towards foreigners and/or foreign languages. In other cases, different cultural settings might have led to differing views among contemporaries. In any event, a negative attitude towards foreign languages does not appear to have been a universally held ideology throughout the histories of each tradition. Nevertheless, when it is found, the parallels between its instantiation in the Hebrew and Arabic grammatical traditions are striking.

3.1. Hebrew Grammarians

Blaming foreign languages, especially Aramaic and Arabic, for the decline of proper Hebrew among the people is a common theme among Hebrew grammarians like Saadia and al-Qirqisānī. Other grammarians like Ibn Qurayš, however, have a much more positive view of foreign languages like Aramaic and Arabic and their value for understanding Biblical Hebrew.

3.1.1. Saadia Gaon (882–942 CE)

As we noted in the preceding section (see §2.1.1), Saadia believed that if *al-umma* 'the nation' and its youth would read and study his grammar book, they would become *faṣīḥ* in the Hebrew language; thus, the prophetic verse from Isaiah (32.4) would be fulfilled. The Hebrew text of Isaiah 32.4 reads וּלְבַ֣ב נִמְהָרִ֔ים יָבִ֖ין לָדָ֑עַת וּלְשׁ֣וֹן עִלְּגִ֔ים תְּמַהֵ֖ר לְדַבֵּ֥ר צָחֽוֹת׃ 'And the heart of the hasty will understand knowledge, and the tongue of the stammerers will hasten to speak *ṣɔ̄ḥōṯ*'. Although we called attention earlier to the significance of this verse for Saadia's language ideology—especially as it relates to *ṣɔ̄ḥōṯ* and *faṣāḥa*—we left Saadia's particularly interesting translation choice for the Hebrew word עִלְּגִים *ʿillgīm* 'stammerers' in his *Tafsīr* without further comment; his full translation of the verse reads as follows (Derenbourg 1896, 47):

> וקלוב אלבלדין תפהם אלמערפה̈ ואלסן אלעג̇ם תסרע בכלאם אלפצאחה̈[77]
>
> And the hearts of the stupid will understand knowledge and the tongues of **foreigners (*ʿajam*)** will hasten to speak *al-faṣāḥa.*

In the Hebrew, the flow of the text is such that those who are to speak *ṣɔ̄ḥōṯ* are the very ones who would never be expected to speak *ṣɔ̄ḥōṯ*, namely 'stammerers'. This characteristic reversal of norms is a recurring theme in the prophecies of Isaiah 32. In Saadia's *Tafsīr*, however, the Hebrew word עִלְּגִים *ʿillgīm* is not rendered as 'stammerers' but rather as אלעג̇ם (≈ العجم) 'foreigners'. Had Saadia wanted to indicate 'stammerers' more transparently, he might have used a lexeme like ألكن 'stammerer'.[78] Interestingly, this interpretation is not unique to Saadia, but precisely what al-Fāsī has in his dictionary entry for עלגים *ʿLGYM* (Skoss 1936–1945, II:399).[79] Both Saadia and al-Fāsī, then, see in this

---

[77] ≈ وقلوب البلدين تفهم المعرفة وألسن العجم تسرع بكلام الفصاحة.

[78] Note that, due to his Persian background, Sībawayh himself was called ألكن 'a stammerer' by ʾAbū Mūsā al-Ḥāmiḍ (d. 918 CE) and أعجم لا يفصح 'a non-Arab who does not [speak Arabic] eloquently' by al-Farrāʾ (d. 822/823 CE; Marogy 2010a, 6–7).

[79] It is possible, however, that this interpretation might be influenced by Isa. 28.11, to which al-Fāsī compares this verse.

verse from Isaiah a contrast between *al-ʿajam* 'foreigners' and those who can speak *faṣāḥa*.

It is worth mentioning here that earlier translation traditions were all consistent in translating the word עלגים *ʿLGYM* as something along the lines of 'stammerers'.[80] Therefore, it seems that Saadia may be reading into this verse something of the wider ideological world that he is a part of in which foreigners, rather than mere 'stammerers', are considered the opposite of one who speaks *faṣāḥa*. Saadia's translation in his *Tafsīr* thus provides us with an example of how language ideology does not just affect the way one understands an abstract concept of language itself, but also how one understands meaning within a language.

The fact that Saadia makes such a strong connection between this prophetic verse (Isa. 32.4) and the outcome of his mission—alongside his poignant translation of *ʿillḡīm* as 'foreigners'—ought to raise a number of questions for us. If Saadia's goal was that the *ʿillḡīm* 'stammerers' or *ʿajam* 'foreigners' would speak *faṣāḥa*, who were they? Based on the passage from *Sefer Ha-Galuy* in which he connects his mission to this verse (see §2.1.1), it seems that Saadia regarded the Jewish *umma* itself as the *ʿillḡīm* who, after studying his grammatical works, would fulfil the prophecy and speak the *faṣāḥa* of the language they had formerly 'forgotten'. If this is the case, how did the nation as a whole lose proficiency in a language they once knew? Moreover, does Saa-

[80] The Greek LXX has *αἱ γλῶσσαι αἱ ψελλίζουσαι* 'the stuttering tongues', the Latin Vulgate has *lingua balborum* 'the tongue of stammerers', and the Syriac Peshitta has ܠܫܢܐ ܕܥܠܓܐ 'the tongue of stutterers'.

dia's translation of Isaiah 32.4 in his *Tafsīr* imply that he associated the ineloquent Jewish nation itself with *al-ʿajam* 'foreigners'?

We may find greater insight into the answers to these questions from the portion of the Arabic introduction to *Sefer Ha-Galuy* immediately preceding the passage (see §2.1.1) in which Saadia references this verse from Isaiah (Harkavy 1891, 154–57; Malter 1913, 493, 498):

> ואמא אלת̇ל[א]ת̇ אבואב אלעאמה̈ פהי שאמלה̈ לגמיע אלכתאב אלאול
> מנהא תעלים אלאמה̈ פציח כלאם אלעבראני לאני ראיתה[א] מד̇ גלבת
> עליהא אללגה̈ אלערביה̈ ואלנבטיה̈ בל אלדני מנהמא אנסוהא לגתהא
> אלפציחה̈ וכלאמהא אלבדיע[81]
>
> With respect to the three general parts, they comprise the entire book. The first of them is teaching the nation the *faṣīḥ* of the Hebrew idiom (*kalām al-ʿibrānī*), since I perceived it (i.e., the nation) [in such a state] that ever since the Arabic and Nabatean languages, particularly the inferior of the two, had prevailed over it (i.e., the nation), they caused [the nation] to forget their clear language (*lughatahā al-faṣīḥa*) and their wonderful idiom (*kalāmahā al-badīʿ*).

Although we read earlier that Saadia was grieved at the nation's 'forgetting' the language (see §2.1.1), we were left wondering why or how Saadia believed such 'forgetting' came about in the first place. In this passage Saadia makes clear that the forgetting was not merely due to time or neglect but actually caused

---

81 ≈ وأما الثلاث أبواب العامة فهي شاملة لجميع الكتاب الأول منها تعليم الأمة فصيح كلام العبراني لأني رأيتها مذ غلبت عليها اللغة العربية والنبطية بل الدني منهما أنسوها لغتها الفصيحة وكلامها البديع.

by the predominance of foreign languages. According to Saadia, it was Arabic and Aramaic[82] that אנסוהא (≈ أنسوها) '*caused* [the nation] to forget'. From an ideological perspective, blaming foreign languages for the deterioration of the standard language among the people is one way of bolstering group identity and its association with the standard language (see chapter 3, §2.1.2).

On this point, it is worth noting that, even though the people have forgotten their language and are not proficient in it, Saadia can still refer to it as לגתהא אלפציחה̈ (≈ لغتها الفصيحة) '*their* eloquent language' and כלאמהא אלבדיע (≈ كلامها البديع) '*their* wonderful idiom'. Note also how the term כלאם אלעבראני (≈ كلام العبراني) is reminiscent of the term used in the Arabic grammatical tradition to refer to the corpus of the standard (performance) language (see chapter 4, §2.2). All this points strongly to the idea that Biblical Hebrew is a wonderful cultural possession of the people (see chapter 3, §§2.1.1–2.1.3), even if the influx of foreign languages, such as Arabic and Aramaic, has made them forget it.

This assertion about the influence of foreign languages, however, also raises questions about Saadia's view of the linguistic history of Hebrew. We have already established that a phrase like *lugha faṣīḥa* is not just referring to Hebrew in general, but specifically to the Hebrew characteristic of the Bible. Therefore, we may ask a few important questions: If the Jewish community had already forgotten Biblical Hebrew in Saadia's day, what sort

---

[82] Malter (1921, 271) argues that 'Nabatean' is referring to Aramaic here. Nabatean referring to Aramaic in Saadia's writings is also acknowledged by Maman (2004, 178).

of competence did he imagine that they had before Arabic and Aramaic caused them to lose it? Further, how widespread had this competence been among the people? Finally, how far back in time do we have to go to find a Jewish nation that exemplified such competence?

While not all of these questions may be answered completely, the beginning of Saadia's *Sefer Ha-Egron* provides a partial answer. As we noted earlier (chapter 4, §1.1.1), after the Arabic introduction, the Hebrew of *Sefer Ha-Egron* begins with a short poetic account of the history of Hebrew from creation. Though the world began with just one holy language, the earth was subsequently split, and each people came to have their own language, with Hebrew belonging to the sons of ʿEber. Saadia continues by explaining that when the people came out of Egypt, God addressed them with דִּבְרֵי צְחוֹת *divrē ṣɔ̄ḥōṯ* 'eloquent/clear words', which became an inheritance for them throughout their generations. Indeed, Hebrew was the language of their kings as they commanded tasks, the language of the priests and the Levites as they sang songs in the temple, the language of the prophets as they expressed their visions, and the language of the princes as they spoke wisdom.[83]

This golden age of speaking *ṣɔ̄ḥōṯ* was brought to an end, however, when the Temple was destroyed and the people were exiled to Babylon. It is at this point in Saadia's narrative history

[83] For Saadia's poetic recounting of the history of Hebrew at the beginning of *Sefer Ha-Egron*, see Harkavy (1891, 52–55).

that we begin to find answers to our questions concerning Saadia's belief about how and when foreign languages brought about the 'forgetting' of Hebrew (Harkavy 1891, 54–55):

> בִּשְׁנַת מֵאָה וְאַחַת שָׁנָה לְחַרְבוֹת עִיר־אֱלֹהֵינוּ הֲחִילוֹנוּ לִטּוֹשׁ לְשׁוֹן הַקֹּדֶשׁ וּלְסַפֵּר בִּלְשׁוֹנוֹת עַמֵּי נֵכַר־הָאָרֶץ שָׁלוֹשׁ שָׁנִים לִפְנֵי מְלָךְ־מֶלֶךְ לִבְנֵי יָוָן: בִּימֵי נְחַמְיָהוּ הַפֶּחָה וְכָל־מֵתָיו רָאֹה רָאָנוּ מְדַבְּרִים אַשְׁדּוֹדִית וַיִּחַר לוֹ וַיִּגְעַר בָּעָם וַיָּרֶב בָּם:[84]
>
> In the one hundred and first year after the destruction of the city of our God, we began to abandon the Holy Language and to converse in the languages of the foreign peoples of the land, three years before a king of the Greeks reigned. In the days of Nehemiah the governor and all his men, he plainly beheld us speaking in Ashdodite! He became angry, rebuked the people, and contended with them.

Saadia, of course, is alluding to a particular passage in the biblical book of Nehemiah, in which Nehemiah sees that the people have married foreign wives and rebukes them for it (13.23–25a):

> גַּם ׀ בַּיָּמִים הָהֵם רָאִיתִי אֶת־הַיְּהוּדִים הֹשִׁיבוּ נָשִׁים אשדודיות (ק׳ אַשְׁדֳּדִיּוֹת) עמוניות (ק׳ עַמֳּנִיּוֹת) מוֹאֲבִיּוֹת: וּבְנֵיהֶם חֲצִי מְדַבֵּר אַשְׁדּוֹדִית וְאֵינָם מַכִּירִים לְדַבֵּר יְהוּדִית וְכִלְשׁוֹן עַם וָעָם: וָאָרִיב עִמָּם וָאֲקַלְלֵם
>
> Also in those days I saw the Jews who had taken Ashdodite, Ammonite, and Moabite women as wives to live with them. As for their children, half of them speak Ashdodite and do not know how to speak Judahite! And the same

---

[84] *bi-šnaṯ mēʾɔ v-ʾaḥaṯ šɔnɔ l-ḥarvōṯ ʿīr ʾɛlōhēnū haḥīlōnū liṭṭōš lšōn haqqoḏɛš u-lsappēr bi-lšōnōṯ ʿammē nēḵar hɔ-ʾɔrɛṣ šɔlōš šɔnīm lifnē mlɔḵ mɛlɛḵ li-vnē yɔvɔn. b-īmē nḥamyɔhū hap-pɛḥɔ v-ḵɔl mēṯɔv rɔʾō rɔʾɔnū mḏabbrīm ʾašdōḏīṯ vayyiḥar bɔ-ʿɔm vayyɔrɛv bɔm.*

> goes for the languages of the other peoples [with whom they had intermarried]. So I confronted them and cursed them.

Nehemiah, of course, is dealing with the repatriation of Babylonian Jews back to the Holy Land more than a century after the original exile. After multiple generations in Babylon, the Jewish community there would have learned Aramaic. When they were repatriated to the land of their ancestors over the course of the sixth and fifth centuries BCE, their Hebrew ability would have been diminished. In addition to this, some of the Jews—whether those who remained in the Land or the recent repatriates—had intermarried with neighbouring foreign peoples. As a result of such intermarriage with foreigners, Nehemiah perceives that their children were speaking in foreign languages and could no longer understand Hebrew.

For Saadia, then, the Hebrew Bible itself bears witness to the beginning of the deterioration of *kalām al-ʿibrānī*. It began already in Nehemiah's time due to intermarrying with foreigners who did not speak Hebrew. Echoing the rebuke of Nehemiah almost fourteen hundred years later, Saadia blames foreign languages for making the people forget their clear language and wonderful idiom. In Saadia's day, however, he could not blame Ashdodite, Ammonite, or Moabite for the demise of Hebrew. Rather, he lays the charge at the feet of Arabic and Aramaic, which were the native languages of his contemporaries.[85]

---

[85] Aramaic might also be mentioned because it was the vernacular of many Jews before the Islamic conquests brought Arabic to the region.

It may be this sort of ideological casting of himself as a 'second Nehemiah' that leads him to associate the community with *al-ʿajam* 'foreigners' in his use of Isaiah 32.4. It is not a literal appellation, but rather a rebuke for being more knowledgeable in foreign tongues than in Hebrew. In the same mould as the biblical account of Nehemiah, Saadia is pained at the encroachment of foreign tongues and the forgetting of Hebrew. Nevertheless, he does not see a bleak future ahead but believes he will be successful in restoring the *faṣīḥ* of Hebrew to the people, even if they have been more like foreigners in their speech ever since the time of Nehemiah. Longing to restore a linguistic competence to the Jewish nation—a competence which has not been around for more than a millennium—Saadia thus comes to the Jewish community of his time with a prophetic word, אלסן אלעג̇ם תסרע בכלאם אלפצאחה̈ (≈ ألسن العجم تسرع بكلام الفصاحة) 'the tongues of foreigners will hasten to speak eloquence'.

3.1.2. Jacob al-Qirqisānī (first half of 10th c. CE)

A similar ideology regarding foreign languages may also be reflected in a passage from the Karaite scholar al-Qirqisānī's (first half of 10th c. CE) *Kitāb al-anwār wa-l-marāqib* (II.16.2; Nemoy 1939–1945), in which he addresses the issue of whether or not God may be worshipped by different *maḏāhib* 'trends'. He is responding to those who say that اذا جاز أن يتعبد بقراءتين مختلفتين جاز أن يتعبد بمذهبين مختلفين 'if it is permissible for [God] to be worshipped by two reading traditions, it is permissible for him to be worshipped by two trends'.

Rather than affirm that multiple Biblical Hebrew reading traditions are legitimate, he takes the stance that only one reading tradition—the Tiberian reading tradition, localised in Palestine and referred to as قراءة الشأمي ‘the Palestinian/Levantine reading’—is correct and permissible for true worship (Khan 1990). In his effort to ‘delegitimise’ other non-Tiberian reading traditions, he writes the following (II.17.6; Nemoy 1939–1945):

الأُمَّة لمّا طَالَ مَقَامُهَا بالعراق وما وَرَاهَا من مُدُن الجالية تَنَبَّطَتْ قراءتُهُم اذ كُنَّا نَرَى قراءةَ أهل العراق قريبةً من لغة النبط وكذا أهلُ كل نهايةٍ فإنّا نجد قراءتَهُم تُقَارب اللغة التى نَشَؤُا فيها مثل أهل الحِجَاز واليَمَن فانهم لا يُقيمون בֵּי بل يجعلون مَقَامَهَا בֵּי والعلّة فى ذلك نُشُؤُهُم بين العَرَب وٱعتيادُهم لِلُغَتِهِم اذ ليس فى لغة العرب בֵּי... وكذلك أهل إِصْفَهَان فانك تجد قراءتَهُم كَأَنَّهَا ليست بالعبرانىّ وذلك ايضا لٱعتيادهم للسان الفَارِسِىّ الذى هو أَغْلَظُ أَلْسُن الفُرْس وَأَشَدُّهَا فضاضةً وكذلك ايضا صار الرُّوم لا يُقيمون القَامِصَة لانها ليست فى لغة الرُّومىّ... وكثير من يهود العراق الذى نَشَؤُا بين النبط يجعلون مَقَامَ קדוש קָדִיש...

When the nation’s stay in Iraq and the cities of the Diaspora community beyond it became long, their reading tradition became ‘Nabateanised’ (*tanabbaṭat*). For we see that the reading tradition of the people of Iraq was similar to the language of the Nabateans, and so it was with the people of every remote region, so that we find their reading tradition resembling the language in whose environment they grew up. This is the case with the people of the Ḥijāz and Yemen, in that they cannot pronounce *vē* and instead make it like *bē*. The reason for this is the fact that they have grown up among the Arabs and have grown accustomed to their language, since there is no *vē* in the language of the Arabs... and so it is with the people of Iṣfahān,

> such that you find their reading tradition as if it is not Hebrew. This also is due to the fact that they have grown accustomed to the Persian language, which is the most error-ridden language of the Persians and the most severely fragmented. So also the Byzantines have come to no longer pronounce the *qameṣ* because it is not in the Byzantine language... and many of the Jews of Iraq who grew up among the Nabateans make *qɔ̄ḏōš* into *qɔ̄ḏēš*...

Much of the philology in this passage is not so different from the findings of modern scholars regarding the various reading traditions of Biblical Hebrew in the Middle Ages. Indeed, the phonological inventory of a particular reading tradition generally comes to resemble that of the vernacular (Morag 1958). In this way, al-Qirqisānī's philological analysis is relatively sound, including the examples he proffers, such as /v/ shifting to [b] due to the absence of [v] in Arabic.[86]

What is noteworthy here, however, is the standard language ideology underlying the comparison. The reading tradition of أهل الشأم 'the Palestinians' is the measuring stick against which all other traditions are compared. Where there is divergence, it is the other traditions that are blamed for admitting vernacular influence—not the 'Palestinian' one. Surely changes could not have come about in 'the Land'. Rather, they are the result of the influence of foreign languages like Aramaic, Arabic, Persian, or Greek on the reading traditions of Diaspora communities. This

[86] Note that some modern Yemenite reading traditions of Biblical Hebrew realise *bet rafa* as [b]. In Aden, for example, the word שֶׁבַע *šɛvaʿ* 'seven' is pronounced as [ˈʃabaʕ] (Ya'akov 2015, 25).

ideological preference for the reading tradition of أهل الشأم 'the Palestinians' (i.e., the Tiberian vocalisation) is based at least in part on their geographical presence in 'the Land' (Khan 1990, 65–66).

Al-Qirqisānī's preferential treatment of 'the Land' is made quite clear in his discussion regarding the logical impossibility that God could have spoken to the sons of Israel in two different traditions (II.17.5; Nemoy 1939–1945):

> وهو انه لا يخلو ان يكون خاطبهم بذلك بِلُغَة الشأميّ او بلُغَة العراقيّ فَأَيُّهُمَا
> كان فهى واحدةٌ لا محالة ولا يجوز ان يقال انه خاطبهم بلُغَة العراق لان ذلك
> يُوجب ان يكون بنو إسرائيل وهم فى الأرض قد غَيَّرُوا القراءة وبدّلوها وذلك
> مُحَال اذ كانت الناقلة للقراءة من أهل الشأم على هذا نقلوها وكذلك الرُّوم
> وأهل المَغْرِب الذى هم جاليةُ البيت الثانى قراءتُهُم هى الشأميّ فان قالوا فان
> كان هذا فيجب ان يكون أهل العراق قد غيّروا وبدّلوا

> So God would have had to have spoken to them thus, whether in the language of the Palestinians or in the language of the Iraqis. Whichever of the two it was would thus undoubtedly be the only [correct tradition]. It cannot be said, however, that [God] spoke to them in the language of Iraq since this would imply that the Israelites, while [remaining] in the Land, changed the reading tradition and altered it. Such would be impossible, since the transmission of the reading was done by the Palestinians (i.e., Tiberians) and this is the way they passed it down. This is also the case with the Byzantines and the Moroccans, who are [the descendants of] the exiles of [the period of the destruction of] the Second Temple, whose reading is the Palestinian one. With this being the case, it is therefore the Iraqis who must have changed and altered [the reading].

For al-Qirqisānī, there is just one correct form of the language, which must be tied to the tradents who remained in the Land. The fact that the Land of Israel confers authority, at least in part, to the reading tradition of its inhabitants may reflect something of the tendency for standard language ideologies to associate the 'single uniform language' with group identity (see chapter 3, §2.1.2). While all other reading traditions were corrupted to some extent by the influence of foreign languages, the 'Palestinian' tradition associated with the Land was faithfully transmitted so as to preserve the pure and correct Hebrew.

We should note here, however, that al-Qirqisānī's own philological analysis is biased due to his language ideology. While he is not wrong about the influence of vernacular speech on various reading traditions, he seems to think that no such influence was exerted on the Tiberian tradition. Nevertheless, there are a number of phonological elements of Tiberian that are likely the result of language contact. Note how the shift of original *waw* = /w/ → *vav* = /v/ in an ancestor of Tiberian is itself probably a contact-induced change based on proximity to Greek and Aramaic (Khan and Kantor 2022).

3.1.3. Yehudah ibn Qurayš (ca late 9th/10th c. CE)

Before concluding this section, however, it is worth noting that, even though both Saadia and al-Qirqisānī blame inferior Hebrew on the prevalence of foreign languages, this thought is not echoed across the Hebrew grammatical tradition. Yehudah ibn Qurayš (ca late 9th/10th c. CE), for example, an Algerian lexicographer and one of the earliest comparative Semitic philologists, exhibits a much more favourable view of Arabic and Aramaic in his letter to the Jews in Fās.

Rather than tell the people that Arabic and Aramaic are responsible for the decline of Hebrew, he actually upbraids them for neglecting the Aramaic *Targum* (i.e., translation) of the Bible. According to Ibn Qurayš, the Jews' ancestors, the ancients—he uses the phrase אואילכם... אבאוכם (≈ أوائلكم... آباؤكم) 'your people of former times... your fathers'—were not ignorant of its benefit and did not neglect its study. He goes on to say that Aramaic and Arabic are actually necessary to understand Biblical Hebrew. In most marked contrast to al-Qirqisānī, he even goes so far as to call attention to the fact that the language of the Bible itself has Aramaic and Arabic words mixed in with it (Becker 1984, 116–17):

> גׄמיע לשון קדש אלחאצל פי אלמקרא קד אנתְתַׄרת פיה אלפאטׄ סריאניה ואכתלטת בה לגה ערביה ותשדׄרת פיה חרוף עגׄמיה וברבריה ולא סימא אלערביה כׄאצה פאן פיהא כתיר מן גׄריב אלפאטׄהא וגׄדנאה עבראניא מחצׄא חתי לא יכון בין אלעבראני ואלערבי פי דלך מן אלאכתלאף אלא מא בין אבתדאל אלצאד ואלצׄאד ואלגימל ואלגׄים ואלטת ואלטׄא ואלעין ואלגַׄין ואלחֵא ואלכׄא ואלזאי ואלדׄאל...[87]
>
> All 'the Holy Language' which occurs in the Bible has Aramaic words scattered within it, Arabic language mixed in

87 ≈ جميع לשון קדש الحاصل في المقرأ قد انتشرت فيه ألفاظ سريانية واختلطت به لغة عربية وتشذرت فيه حروف عجمية وبربرية ولا سيما العربية خاصة فإن فيها كثير من غريب ألفاظها وجدناه عبرانيا محضا حتى لا يكون بين العبراني والعربي في ذلك من الاختلاف إلا ما بين ابتدال ال-צאד والضاد وال-גימל والجيم وال-טת والظاء وال-עין والغين وال-חֵא والخاء وال-זאי والذال.

> with it, and foreign and Berber forms dispersed within it. This is especially the case with Arabic in particular, for we have found that many of its obscure words are actually pure Hebrew, so that there is not really a difference in such cases between Hebrew and Arabic, provided that you substitute *ṣād* with *ḍād*, *gimel* with *jīm*, *ṭet* with *ẓāʾ*, *ʿayin* with *ghayn*, *ḥāʾ with ḫāʾ*, and *zay* with *ḏāl*...

While al-Qirqisānī focuses on a pure Biblical Hebrew reading tradition, which is negatively influenced by the phonology of foreign languages, Yehudah ibn Qurayš focuses on the benefits that comparative language study can have in unlocking some of the obscure lexicon of the Hebrew Bible. Even if their respective ideologies are not necessarily contradictory—one focuses on the phonology of a reading tradition and the other on comparative lexical work—their vastly different stance towards foreign languages is apparent.

Yehudah ibn Qurayš's more positive view towards foreign languages may be due to the fact that, in his cultural context, Aramaic still enjoyed a relatively significant level of prestige, which it eventually relinquished to Arabic as the latter became more predominant.[88] Even though Aramaic was no longer spoken as an everyday vernacular, scholars like Ibn Qurayš might have viewed Aramaic as a 'cultural possession' similar to Hebrew due to its long historical association with Jewish liturgy and various religious literature. This itself would constitute a significant facet of the grammarians' language ideology.

---

[88] For more on the context of Ibn Qurayš, see Becker (1984); Maman (2010); Sasson (2016).

That apparent Aramaic and Arabic loanwords presented some tension for the language ideology of the Hebrew grammarians has been acknowledged by Maman (2004, 21–32). According to Maman (2004, 28), the idea of loanwords from Aramaic and Arabic in Biblical Hebrew is somewhat hazy among the grammarians. In many cases, the Hebrew grammarians appear to walk a fine line between mere השוואה *hašvɔ̄ʾɔ̄* 'comparison' and outright גזרון *gizzɔ̄rōn* 'etymology' (i.e., derivation).

3.2. Comparison with the Arabic Tradition

The phenomenon of blaming the decline of the nation's language ability on the predominance of foreign languages is quite apparent in the Arabic grammatical tradition as well.

3.2.1. al-Jāḥiẓ (d. 868/869 CE)

In the continuation of the passage from al-Jāḥiẓ's (d. 868/869 CE) *Al-bayān wa-l-tabyīn* examined in our section on the complaint tradition (§2.2.2), al-Jāḥiẓ specifically blames the decline of the language among the people on the influence of foreigners. When explaining how those with improper speech can sometimes only be understood by others who have been around corrupt speech, he writes the following (1.162; Haroun 1998):

وكيف يكون ذلك كلُّه بياناً، ولولا طولُ مخالطة السامع للعجَم وسماعِهِ
للفاسد من الكلام، لما عَرفَه. ونحن لم نَفهم عنه إلا للنَّقص الذى فينا. وأهلُ
هذه اللُّغةِ وأربابُ هذا البيانِ لا يستدلُّون على معانى هؤلاء بكلامهم كما لا
يعرفون رَطانة الرُّوميّ والصَّقلبى، وإن كان هذا الاسم إنّما يستحقُّونه بأنَّا نَفهم
عنهم كثيراً من حوائجهم. فنحن قد نَفهم بحَمْحَمة الفَرَس كثيراً من حاجاته،

ونفهم بضُغاء السِّنَّور كثيراً من إراداته. وكذلك الكلبُ، والحمار، والصبيُّ الرّضيع. وإنّما عنى العتّابى إفهامَكَ العربَ حاجتَك على مَجارى كلام العربِ الفُصَحاء

But how can all of this be elegant expression (*bayān*)? If not for the hearer having spent a long time intermingling with foreigners (*al-ʿajam*) and listening to those who are corrupt in speech, he would not have known it. As for us, we would not have understood what was said except by reason of our own deficiency. Experts in this language and masters of this elegant expression (*bayān*), on the other hand, are unable to infer the meanings of these people in their speech, just as they do not understand the gibberish of the Byzantine and the 'Slav'. And if they only deserve this moniker [of being called 'eloquent'] because we understand many of their needs from what they say, then we might also [mention the fact that] we can understand many of the horse's needs from its neighing, many of the cat's wants from its meowing, and thus also the dog, the donkey, and the breast-feeding child, [but we would not call them eloquent]. What al-ʿAttābī means [with respect to his earlier statement that making someone understand your need constitutes eloquence] is your ability to make the Arabs understand your need according to the manner of speech of the eloquent Arabs (*kalām al-ʿarab al-fuṣaḥāʾ*).

In the beginning portion of this passage quoted earlier (§2.2.2), al-Jāḥiẓ makes the point that eloquent speech is not just about being understood. He continues to drive this point home here with a rather extreme analogy, by which he compares the speech of one who has intermingled with foreigners to the sounds that animals or infants make. Even if one can understand what they want from their utterances, this does not mean that their speech is in any way proper or eloquent. Moreover, those with the purest of speech might not be able to understand them. Communicating with the Arabs is not just about conveying one's needs but doing so in such a way that comports with مجاري كلام العرب الفصحاء 'the manner of speech of the eloquent Arabs', for the most eloquent might only understand the needs of one who speaks eloquently.

Particularly noteworthy here is the fact that طول مخالطة... للعجم 'a long time intermingling with foreigners' is specifically blamed for the corruption of one's speech. Moreover, the speech of foreigners is referred to as رطانة 'gibberish'. These sentiments appear to be tied up with al-Jāḥiẓ's conception that the Bedouin of the desert—especially those of the distant past—are the locale of pure Arabic. Intermingling with foreigners (or non-pure-Arabic speakers) in urban environments is thus the principal cause of linguistic error (Webb 2016, 299–300).

3.2.2. Abū Naṣr al-Fārābī (d. 950 CE)

Though not strictly a grammarian, the Islamic philosopher Abū Naṣr al-Fārābī (d. 950 CE), when discussing the reliability of linguistic data supplied by various sources (i.e., tribes) for grammatical work—namely those not contaminated by *laḥn*—writes the following (text in Qāsim 1976, 56–57; Fajāl 1989, 91–92; analysis and translation in consultation with Suleiman 1999, 22–23; 2003, 51–55; 2011, 6–8; Webb 2016, 311–12):

فإنه لم يُؤْخَذْ لا مِنْ لَخْم، ولا من جُذام؛ فإنهم كانوا مجاورين لأهل مصر، والقِبْطِ، ولا من قُضَاعَة، ولا من غَسَّان، ولا من إياد؛ فإنهم كانوا مجاورين لأهل الشام، وأكثرُهم نصارىٰ يقرؤون في صلاتهم بغير العربية، ولا مِنْ تغْلِب

والنَّمِر، فإنهم كانوا بالجزيرة مجاورين لليونانية، ولا من بَكْر؛ لأنهم كانوا مجاورين للنبَط والفرس، ولا من عبد القيس؛ لأنهم كانوا سُكان البَحْرَيْنِ، مخالطين للهند والفرس، ولا مِنْ أَزْد عمان؛ لمخالطتهم للهِنْد والفُرس، ولا مِنْ أهلِ اليمن أصلًا؛ لمخالطتهم للهند والحبشة، ولولادة الحبشة فيهم، ولا مِنْ بني حَنيفة وسكان اليمامة، ولا مِنْ ثَقِيف وسكان الطائف؛ لمخالطتهم تجّار الأمم المقيمين عندهم، ولا مِنْ حاضرة الحجاز؛ لأن الذين نَقَلُوا اللغة صادفوهم حين ابتدأوا ينقلون لغةَ العرب قد خالطوا غيرَهم من الأمم، وفسدتْ أَلْسِنَتُهُمْ. والذي نَقَلَ اللغةَ واللسانَ العربيَّ عن هؤلاء، وأَثْبَتَهَا في كتاب، وصَيَّرهَا عِلْماً وصناعةً، هم أهلُ الكوفة والبصرةِ فقط، مِنْ بين أمصار العرب[89]

[Linguistic data] were not taken from Laḫm or Juḏām, because they neighboured the people of Egypt and the Copts, nor from Quḍāʿa, Ghassān, or Iyād, because they neighboured the people of Syria, most of whom were Christians who would recite their prayers in languages other than Arabic, nor from Taghlib and Namir, because they were in the Peninsula neighbouring Greek, nor from Bakr, because they neighboured the Nabateans and the Persians, nor from ʿAbd al-Qays, because they were inhabitants of Bahrain and thus intermingled with the Indians and the Persians, nor from Azd of ʿUmān due to their intermingling with the Indians and the Persians, nor at all from the people of Yemen due to their intermingling with the Indians and the Ethiopians, and because the Ethiopians were born amongst them, nor from Banū Ḥanīfa or the inhabitants of Yamāma, nor from Thaqīf or the inhabitants of Ṭāʾif due to their intermingling with the merchants of the nations

[89] For a slightly different version of this text, see al-Mawlā et al. (1998, 212).

> who resided among them, nor from the towns of the Ḥijāz, because the tradents of the language, when they first began to transmit the language of the Arabs (*lughat al-ʿarab*), encountered those who had mixed with those of foreign nations (*ghayrahum min al-umam*), their languages thus being corrupted. Those who transmitted the language (*al-lugha*), that is the Arabic language (*al-lisān al-ʿarabī*), from these [earlier tradents], codified it, and made it into a branch of knowledge (*ʿilm*) and an industry (*ṣināʿa*), are the Kūfans and the Baṣrans alone, from among the cities of the Arabs.

This passage seems to reflect a belief that language contact with foreign influences is the primary cause of *laḥn* in the tribal varieties of Arabic among different speech communities. Those without significant contact with non-Arabic languages were regarded as the most free from *laḥn*. This negative attitude towards language contact also reinforces the value of the Bedouin, who were isolated from the influence of foreign languages out in the desert (Suleiman 1999, 22–23; 2003, 51–55; 2011, 6–8). We should also note here just how similarly this passage reads to that of al-Qirqisānī, a contemporary of al-Fārābī, in his discussion of the corruption of Biblical Hebrew reading traditions among communities outside of Israel (§3.1.2). This similarity is especially striking in the fact that both of these authors specifically name the relevant contact languages negatively influencing the language variety (or reading tradition) of each tribe (or speech community).

3.2.3. Abū al-Ṭayyib al-Lughawī (d. 962 CE)

In the previous section on the 'complaint tradition' (see §2.2.1), we recounted Ibn Sallām's narrative about Abū al-Aswad al-

Duʾalī composing the first grammar of *al-ʿarabiyya* as a result of *kalām al-ʿarab* becoming disturbed due to a preoccupation with the Islamic conquests. Brustad (2016, 154) points out, however, that this story changes somewhat when it is recounted almost a century later in the Arabic grammarian Abū al-Ṭayyib al-Lughawī's (d. 962 CE) *Marātib al-naḥwiyyīn* (Ibrāhīm 1974/2009, 19):

> واعلمْ أنّ أولَ ما اختلَّ من كلام العرب فأَحوجَ إلى التعلّم الإعرابُ، لأن اللّحْن ظهر في كلام الموالي والمتعربين من عهد النبي صلى الله عليه وسلم؛ فقد روينا أن رجلاً لحن بحضرته فقال: «أرشِدوا أخاكم. فقد ضلّ»
>
> And know that the first [element] of *kalām al-ʿarab* that became defective and was thus in greatest need of instruction was *iʿrāb* (i.e., inflectional endings), since grammatical error had appeared in the *kalām* of the *mawālī* and those who had integrated into Arab culture during the time of the prophet, peace of God upon him. And we have reported that when a man committed a grammatical error in his presence, [Muhammad] said, "Guide your brother, for he has erred."

Like Ibn Sallām, Abū al-Ṭayyib al-Lughawī seems to be concerned with the fact that *kalām al-ʿarab* became 'defective'. While both grammarians agree on this point, Brustad (2016, 154) points out that they give different explanations as to why it became defective. While Ibn Sallām cites the advent of Islam and the Islamic conquests as the reason for *kalām al-ʿarab* becoming defective (see §2.2.1), Abū al-Ṭayyib al-Lughawī blames it on the influx of foreign languages. Note that the two groups he blames for the corruption of the language, *al-mawālī* and *al-mutaʿarribūn*, are characteristically 'non-Arab' populations. It is also significant to note that the feature most characteristically associated with *kalām al-ʿarab*—or at least the lack thereof with its deterioration—is *iʿrāb*.

3.2.4. al-Zubaydī (d. 989 CE)

A similar shift of blame from a preoccupation with the Islamic conquests to an influx of foreigners is also found in al-Zubaydī's (d. 989 CE) account of this story (*Ṭabaqāt al-naḥwiyyīn wa-l-lughawiyyīn*; Ibrāhīm 1973, 22):

> قال: أولُ من وضع العربية أبو الأسود الدؤليّ، جاء إلى زياد بالبصرة، فقال: إنى أرى العرب قد خالطت هذه الأعاجم، وتغيّرت ألسنتُهم، أفتأذن لى أن أضع للعرب كلاماً يقيمون به كلامهم؟ قال: لا، فجاء رجل إلى زياد، فقال: أصلح اللّه الأمير! توفى أبانا وترك بنون. فقال زياد: تُوفى أبانا وترك بنون! ادع لى أبا الأسود. فقال: ضع للناس الذى كنت نهيتُك أن تضع لهم

> [ʿĀṣim ibn Abī al-Najūd] said: "The first one who codified the *ʿarabiyya* was Abū al-Aswad al-Duʾalī. He came to Ziyād in Baṣra and said, 'For I see that the Arabs have intermingled with these foreigners/non-Arabic speakers (*al-aʿājim*) and their languages have changed. So will you permit me to codify for the Arabs a *kalām* upon which they will base their *kalām*?' He said, 'No.' Then a man came to Ziyād and said, 'May God keep well the governor! Our father (*abānā.ACC*) has died and left behind children (*banūn.NOM*).' Ziyād said, 'Our father (*abānā.ACC*) has died and left behind children (*banūn.NOM*)!? Call for me Abū al-Aswad.' So [after he came, Ziyād] said [to him], 'Compose/codify for the people [the book] that you had intended to compose/codify for them.'"

Once again, we see that in a tenth-century source—in contrast to Ibn Sallām's ninth-century account—intermingling with non-Arabs and foreign languages are blamed for the deterioration of *al-ʿarabiyya*, rather than preoccupation with the Islamic conquests. This may indicate that the ideology that saw foreign languages as responsible for the deterioration of pure Arabic developed over time in the Arabic grammatical tradition.

Also worth noticing here is the specific type of grammatical error exemplified in this fanciful story that al-Zubaydī recounts to make his point. After the governor initially fails to see the need for al-Duʾalī's grammar project, he immediately reverses course when a man comes before him and confuses the nominative and accusative case multiple times in just a four-word announcement of his father's death. This may tie in with the idea that *iʿrāb* and the case inflectional system were regarded as the most characteristic features of *al-ʿarabiyya*.

3.2.5. al-Khalīl ibn Aḥmad (d. 786/791 CE)

Nevertheless, even if the ideology that *al-ʿarabiyya* became defective due to the influx of non-Arabs and foreign languages was a later development in the tradition, the seeds for the association of foreigners and ineloquence seem to have been around earlier. Note, for example, the explanation that al-Khalīl (d. 786/791 CE) provides for the word *ʿajam* in his dictionary *Kitāb al-ʿayn* (1.237; al-Makhzūmī and al-Sāmarrāʾī 1989):

العَجَمُ: ضِدُّ العَرَب. ورجلٌ أعجميّ: ليس بعربيّ وقوم عجم وعرب والأعجم: الذي لا يُفْصِحُ

Al-ʿajam: the opposite of Arabs (*ʿarab*). And an *aʿjamī* man: not an Arab (*ʿarabī*). And a group (i.e., plural): *ʿajam* and Arabs (*ʿarab*). And *al-aʿjam*: one who does not speak eloquently (*lā yufṣiḥu*).

We should first of all note that there may be some morphosemantic differences between the terms *ʿajam* and *aʿjam*. Note, for example, that in the later lexicographer al-Azharī's (d. 980 CE) *Tahḏīb al-lugha* we find a distinction between ethnic *ʿajamī* (i.e., 'foreigner') and linguistic *aʿjamī* ('one of improper speech'). According to Webb (2016, 180–81), however, this reflects a later conceptualistion concomitant with a shift in thought from seeing *ʿarab* as a primarily linguistic term to a primarily ethnic term. In fact, in the context here, both *ʿajam* and *aʿjamī* are set up as the opposite of *ʿarab*. This would seem to point to at least some contrast between *al-ʿajam* 'non-Arabic speakers → foreigners' and *al-faṣāḥa* 'eloquence' in the Arabic grammatical tradition. At the same time, however, we do not want to flatten diachronic development within the Arabic lexical tradition. If at an early period, like that of al-Khalīl, the term *ʿarab* referred merely to a linguistic community—i.e., speakers of (pure) Arabic—rather than an ethnic one (Webb 2016, 178–79), then the opposition with *ʿajam* is not as ethnically charged. This lexical entry would only be contrasting speakers of pure Arabic with those who do not speak clearly.

It is only when reading lexical entries like this through the lens of the later grammarians, during whose time *ʿarab* was clearly an ethnic term (Webb 2016, 178), that this opposition has such strong ethnic connotations. Nevertheless, reading earlier grammatical texts—or interacting with earlier grammatical and cultural traditions—through the lens of later grammarians is perhaps precisely how the ideology we are considering developed in the first place. If the terms *ʿarab* and *ʿajam* were originally more linguistically based, then re-reading such lexical entries in later centuries, after these terms had become more ethnically connoted, would indeed have resulted in a contrast between *al-ʿajam* 'foreigners' and *al-faṣāḥa* 'eloquence'. If such is the case, it is not hard to imagine how this single example could represent a microcosm of a wider societal shift.

3.3. Analysis

As we demonstrated in the preceding section, in both the Hebrew and Arabic grammatical traditions, the emergence of grammar is couched within the context of the complaint tradition (see §2.0). It is witnessing the linguistic ineptitude of the masses that moves the grammarians to compose their grammatical works.

Over time, however, this complaint tradition regarding the deterioration of 'pure' language among the masses takes on other aspects. In particular, foreign languages and/or the influx of foreigners are blamed for the neglect of the standard language. In the case of Saadia, deterioration of pure Hebrew is the result of the prevalence of Aramaic and Arabic. For him, this problem goes as far back as the time of Nehemiah, in whose mould he casts himself as one passionate for the purity of the language coming to restore eloquence to the nation. Al-Qirqisānī similarly delegitimises non-'Palestinian' (i.e., non-Tiberian) reading traditions due to their being influenced by the vernacular languages of their tradents, naming specific examples of negative language contact. In the Arabic tradition, Abū al-Ṭayyib al-Lughawī sees grammar emerging after linguistic error began to appear in the speech of non-Arabs, namely the *mawālī* and those who had integrated into Arab culture. Al-Zubaydī likewise recounts how the language changed as a result of intermingling with foreigners; this prompted al-Du'alī to first codify the grammar of the language. Others, like al-Jāḥiẓ and al-Fārābī, blame the corruption of pure Arabic on language contact with foreigners. The passage cited from al-Fārābī, in particular, exhibits striking similarity with that of al-Qirqisānī, his contemporary, in that various contact languages, which he specifically and extensively lists, are decried for their negative influence.

From a linguistic ideological perspective, a negative attitude towards foreign languages and their influence can serve to buttress associations between the standard canonical language and group identity (see chapter 3, §2.1.2). This may even be reflected in the dictionary entries of al-Fāsī in the Hebrew grammatical tradition and al-Khalīl in the Arabic grammatical tradition, who appear to cast foreigners as the opposite of eloquent users of the language.

For some of the grammarians, historicisation also becomes a major component of this attitude towards foreign languages. As we noted above, standard language cultures often regard only the canonical form as having a substantial, continuous, pure, and thus authoritative history. Variant forms of the language must thus be regarded as substandard degenerate forms. In many cases, foreign language influence is seen as a major contributing factor to such degeneracy (see chapter 3, §2.1.2). This ideological framework appears to cohere with al-Qirqisānī's perception of reading traditions that developed outside of Palestine and al-Fārābī's perception of Arabic varieties that developed outside of an isolated (from foreign influence) context. In Saadia, historicisation goes even further, so that it is not only the standard language that is given a long and ancient history, but the negative influence of foreign languages as well. In this way, he even historicises the conflict with foreign languages itself and thus also his role as restorer in the face of such a linguistic crisis.

It is curious, however, that blaming foreign languages for the deterioration of the standard language is not evidenced at all times and in all places in each of the traditions. In the earliest sources of the Arabic tradition, such as Ibn Sallām (d. 845/846 CE), foreign languages are not necessarily blamed for the deterioration of the standard language. On the other hand, in later ninth- and tenth-century sources, such as al-Jāḥiẓ (d. 868/869 CE), al-Fārābī (d. 950 CE), Abū al-Ṭayyib (d. 962 CE), and al-Zubaydī (d. 989 CE), the lack of eloquence of the people is blamed on the influence of foreign languages and/or the influx of foreigners.

In the Hebrew grammatical tradition, chronology seems to be less significant, since contemporaries may hold differing views. While Saadia (d. 942 CE) and al-Qirqisānī (first half of 10th c. CE) exhibit negative attitudes towards foreign languages and their influence on Hebrew, Ibn Qurayš (d. 10th c. CE) expresses a more positive opinion regarding their usefulness for biblical study. The reason for Ibn Qurayš's distinctly positive view on foreign languages as opposed to his contemporaries is not immediately obvious. It may be that Aramaic was viewed as more of a 'cultural possession' for Ibn Qurayš. Saadia and al-Qirqisānī, on the other hand, might have been more exposed in their (cultural, societal, geographical, etc.) contexts to the Arabic grammarians—and thus more subjected to the influence of their standard language ideology. In any case, while it lies beyond the scope of the present work to fully account for the different attitude of Ibn Qurayš,[90] we may nevertheless highlight the fact that the ideology regarding foreign languages reflected in Saadia and al-Qirqisānī exhibits close parallels with that of the Arabic grammarians.

---

[90] A linguistic-anthropological treatment of Ibn Qurayš that is sensitive to language ideology in his context is a *desideratum* for future research.

6. CONCLUSIONS

This book is not meant to be a comprehensive treatment of the language ideology of the medieval Hebrew grammarians who wrote in Judeo-Arabic. Nor does it even remotely attempt to be a substantial treatment of the language ideology of the Arabic grammarians of the Middle Ages. What we have focused on are lines of striking similarity between the language ideologies of the respective traditions during the ʿAbbasid period: language as a cultural possession (see chapter 4, §1.0), proper language determined by an ancient corpus (see chapter 4, §2.0), the 'fieldwork' *topos* (see chapter 4, §3.0), a performative register of language (see chapter 5, §1.0), the complaint tradition (see chapter 5, §2.0), and a negative attitude towards foreign languages (see chapter 5, §3.0).

These trends all serve to maintain and perpetuate a cohesive standard language ideology. By referring to the language as belonging to the 'Hebrews' or 'Arabs' (see chapter 4, §1.0), the language is affirmed as a cultural possession (see chapter 3, §2.1.1). Nevertheless, at least in the period during which most of the grammarians examined in this book conducted their work, these monikers refer not to the grammarians' contemporaries but rather to exemplary speakers of the past and ancient (sacred) corpora. The standard language is thus historicised (see chapter 3, §2.1.8) and conceived of as an abstract entity that exists outside of native speakers (see chapter 3, §2.1.3); as such, its proper form must be learned. The grammarians must thus make judgments regarding 'correct' or 'proper' language use (see chapter 4, §2.0).

 https://doi.org/10.11647/OBP.0382.06

The role of the grammarian as language evaluator also implicitly serves to guide the process of enregisterment with respect to what and whom should be elevated as exemplary sources and speakers. One notable element in which this becomes instantiated is the 'fieldwork' *topos* in which the grammarians must venture out into a particular setting to collect linguistic examples from exemplary speakers among the commonfolk of a particular demographic, whether those chatting in the streets of Tiberias or the Bedouin of the desert (see chapter 4, §3.0). Overall, however, exemplary sources are characterised by the linguistic style of the ancient corpus, which is associated with performance language found in sacred texts, poetry, and speeches (see chapter 3, §3.0; chapter 5, §1.0). Someone proficient in the linguistic register of the sacred text (and ancient corpus) is thus regarded *faṣīḥ*. When surveying their own nation in the present day, however, the grammarians express grief at the widespread neglect of the language, as in the 'complaint tradition' (see chapter 3, §§2.1.4–2.1.5; chapter 5, §2.0). The emergence of grammar, which is a form of 'maintenance' of the standard language (see chapter 3, §§2.1.6–2.1.7), comes as a response to such widespread neglect. Over time, this complaint tradition takes on an ethnic sentiment (see chapter 3, §2.1.2), in which the influx of foreigners and/or foreign languages are regarded as a threat and negative influence on the purity of the standard language (see chapter 5, §3.0).

Such lines of similarity could have come about in a variety of ways. While they might be the result of direct influence or a wider shared cultural framework, it is also possible that they merely reflect general trends common in standard language cultures. After all, the whole idea of a culture being possessed of a standard language ideology is that it can be characterised by a number of particular trends that arise in such settings. The idea that the language of a sacred text is treated as a cultural possession, for example, is hardly unique to Jewish or Arab culture. The same applies to complaining that the wider population has neglected the canonical standard language of the society. In fact, this is probably the case for most general aspects of a shared standard language ideology treated in this book.

At the same time, however, we should not overlook the specific details of how these six similar elements of a standard language ideology were instantiated in each of the societies. When we consider how sharply the ideology of the Hebrew grammarians often mirrors that of the Arabic grammarians, it would be plausible to posit at least a shared cultural framework—if not direct influence—as the best explanation for the similarity. Indeed, sometimes the specific instantiation of an element of standard language ideology is just too similar to be chalked up to mere parallel development. This is especially the case when the shared ideology of the Hebrew and Arabic grammarians of the ʿAbbasid period appears to conflict with the ideology of earlier Hebrew poets, etc. Indeed, there are at least several cases where we may suggest that the language ideology evidenced in the Arabic grammarians was transferred to and/or absorbed by the Hebrew grammarians who wrote in Judeo-Arabic during the ʿAbbasid period.

First, although the idea that the language of a sacred text would be a cultural possession and its grammar set the standard for exemplary speakers is not unique to Jewish or Arab culture, the way in which this ideology takes shape and comes to be presented in the Hebrew grammarians is telling in a number of respects. When the grammarian has to judge which non-biblical poetry is eloquent, the specific language used—right down to the verbal root—exhibits a high degree of similarity across the traditions. Saadia, for example, may choose to cite someone מן כאן קולה **מרצ̇יא** (≈ من كان قوله مرضيا) 'whose saying **was pleasing**' and Sībawayh hears linguistic examples ممن ترضى عربيته 'from one whose Arabic **is pleasing**' (see chapter 4, §§1.0–2.0).

Moreover, the ideology surrounding what is determined by the Hebrew grammarians as acceptable or eloquent language for Hebrew poetry may also reflect influence from the ideology of the Arabic tradition. Prior to the emergence of Hebrew grammar towards the end of the first millennium, there was already a thriving and dynamic liturgical poetic tradition known as *piyyuṭ*. Although it was similar to Biblical Hebrew or Rabbinic Hebrew in many ways, it had its own distinct style that continued to develop over time. Some of its most characteristic non-biblical elements include regular rhyme and the extension of rare analogically derived morphology (Rand 2013; Rand 2014). It is striking, then, when Hebrew grammarians like Ḥayyūj correct 'mistakes' in the analogically formed conjugations of weak verbs (chapter 5, §2.1.2), which otherwise might be at home in *piyyuṭ*. Moreover, even though Saadia is willing on occasion to praise the poetry of famous *payṭanim* (e.g., Yose ben Yose, Yannai, Eleazar, Yehoshua, Phinehas), his own idea of what constitutes the best poetry is clearly characterised by a close imitation of biblical style (see chapter 4, §2.1.3; chapter 5, §2.1.1). This movement away from a more diverse poetic tradition to stricter imitation of biblical style may be due to the influence of the ideology of the Arabic tradition, in which the *Qurʾān* and pre-Islamic poetry—though not without internal diversity, much more alike than Biblical Hebrew and *Payṭanic* Hebrew—serve as the corpus for the standard language. This may have swayed some of the Hebrew grammarians to an ideology that required poetry be composed in the 'classical' language.

Second, although a variety of opinions exist regarding the so-called 'fieldwork' motif exhibited in ʿEli ben Yehudah ha-Nazir, a strong case has been made that it is at least partly influenced by the literary *topos* attested in the Arabic tradition of seeking Bedouin informants in the desert. Even if ʿEli ben Yehudah was merely listening to a Hebrew component in the Aramaic vernacular and Hebrew liturgical recitation, he still frames his 'fieldwork' as sitting פי סאחאת טבריה̇ ושוארעהא (≈ في ساحات طبرية وشوارعها) 'in the squares and streets of Tiberias' and listening to כלאם אלסוקה ואלעאמה (≈ كلام السوقة والعامة) 'the speech of the commonfolk and the general populace'. It is thus the elevation of the linguistic prestige of the commonfolk of a particular demographic—rather than that of scholars—that may reflect some infiltration of the literary *topos* of the Arabic tradition. Just as the Arabic grammarians elevate the linguistic status of the Bedouin, so too ʿEli ben Yehudah ha-Nazir and other Hebrew grammarians set up the commonfolk of Tiberias as an exemplary source for linguistic data. In each tradition, the geography of the respective locales is even credited for the pure language of their inhabitants (see chapter 4, §3.0).

Third, even though the practical purpose of the Hebrew grammarians' work was biblical literacy, they sometimes frame their work as addressing deficiencies in a productive performance language culture. On occasion, such framings resemble how the Arabic grammatical tradition presents the performance language culture of *kalām al-ʿarab*. Note that the contexts in which the people make grammatical errors with weak verbs cited by Ḥayyūj (see chapter 5, §1.1.2), namely في خطبهم وأشعارهم 'in their speeches and poems', is reminiscent of al-Khalīl's association of *kalām al-ʿarab* with أشعار 'poems', أمثال 'proverbs', and مخاطبات 'formal speeches' (see chapter 5, §1.2.1). In reality, Hebrew speeches delivered in the synagogue and liturgical poetry were probably closer in style to Rabbinic Hebrew and *Payṭanic* Hebrew than Biblical Hebrew—and had been for a long time. The sudden emphasis on conforming speeches and poetry to biblical style might thus be a result of exposure to the Arabic grammatical tradition. In other words, while associating *al-ʿarabiyya* with contemporary performance contexts was a more organic element of Arabic language ideology, expecting productive performances in Biblical Hebrew style marked a sudden shift in what the linguistic practice and expectations of the Hebrew tradition had been for many centuries. This sudden shift may thus betray the strong presence of language ideologies endemic to the Arabic tradition. Though not afforded much more than a passing comment in the present book, the trend of advocating for everyday speech to be carried out in the standard language—or lamenting that it was not—is also relevant for this point.

Fourth, and finally, while the complaint tradition is common in standard language cultures, there are a few elements of its instantiation in the Hebrew and Arabic grammatical traditions that likely point to ideological influence of the latter on the former. In each tradition, the emergence of grammar is presented as a response to the deterioration or neglect of the standard language in performance contexts. The grammarians thus seek to restore to the people their bygone *faṣāḥa* 'eloquence'—synonymous with the linguistic register and style of the 'classical' language (see chapter 5, §2.0). Moreover, in the writings of numerous of the Hebrew and Arabic grammarians, the complaint tradition takes on an additional aspect in which neglect of the language is blamed on the influx of foreigners and/or foreign languages (see chapter 5, §3.0). In both traditions, we even find a lexical opposition between *ʿajam* 'foreigners' and *fuṣaḥāʾ* 'those that are eloquent'. While a negative attitude towards foreign languages is common in standard language cultures, the close parallels between the two traditions are striking.

Perhaps the most obvious evidence of Arabic ideological influence in the complaint tradition, however, is found in a passage from *Sefer Ha-Egron*. There, Saadia himself references an Arabic grammarian—possibly Abū al-ʿAbbās Aḥmad ibn Yaḥyā, also known as Thaʿlab (d. 904 CE)—not as a source for terminology, concepts, or theory, but rather as analogous to his own context and mission (see chapter 5, §2.1.1). At the very least in this example, then, we have direct evidence of an Arabic grammarian influencing how a Hebrew grammarian conceives of and presents his own work within his own context.

We know that the Hebrew grammarians regularly read and utilised the Arabic grammarians in their own writings (see chapter 2, §2.0), even if much of the work done in this area has focused on grammatical terms and concepts. It is entirely plausible, then, that the striking ideological similarities covered in this short book indicate that elements of the Arabic grammatical tradition absorbed into the Hebrew grammatical tradition include not only terms and concepts but a culture and language ideology as well.

We should be cautious, however, in drawing too many conclusions from the selective comparison presented in this book, which is by no means comprehensive. Given the scope of the present work, it would be difficult to prove anything more than that the Hebrew and Arabic grammarians of the ʿAbbasid period had a similar or shared cultural framework regarding language. Proving direct influence would require a much more careful historical analysis of the social, cultural, and educational contexts of each of the grammarians treated. It would also likely have to consider a rich diversity of ideologies within each tradition. Nevertheless, the present work has called attention to important aspects of a standard language ideology that appear to be shared, right down to nuanced details, between the Hebrew and Arabic grammatical traditions.

Given the increasing interest in the relevance of language ideology for its impact on academic research, we should also consider how the discipline of Hebrew Grammar—as we moderns have inherited it—might still bear the imprint of the medieval Hebrew grammarians' language ideology. The treatment of loanwords, the description of verbal morphology with analogical root variation, and the systematisation of internal linguistic diversity are a few examples in which this impact may still be felt. That Biblical Hebrew has seen far more grammatical treatments published on it than either *Payṭanic* or Medieval Hebrew may also, to an extent, be traced back to the Hebrew grammarians' standard language ideology.

The presentation of 'Biblical Hebrew' as a uniform entity may also be regarded as ideologically driven, given the internal diversity within the corpus and the rich diversity of oral reading traditions. In fact, the equivalence drawn between the Tiberian vocalisation tradition and 'Biblical Hebrew' is itself a legacy of the standard language ideology of medieval Hebrew grammarians like Ḥayyūj. That modern translations of the Bible are based on the Tiberian vocalisation rather than the Babylonian vocalisation is also, at least in part, due to the language ideology of scholars who thought like al-Qirqisānī. That most students and scholars in Biblical Studies rely primarily on the Tiberian tradition for their research is also a fruit of this inherited culture.

Endeavouring to understand the language ideology and culture of the medieval Hebrew grammarians is thus not merely an academic exercise meant to shed light on the thought patterns of medieval scholars. Rather, given the unbroken link between the medieval Hebrew grammarians, early modern grammars like that of Gesenius, and contemporary Biblical Hebrew grammars and linguistic research, we should also constantly be considering how the legacy of the medieval Hebrew grammarians' language ideology might be part of our own academic inheritance as well.

WORKS CITED

Abdel-Tawāb 1982—see al-Kisāʾī.

Agha, Asif. 2003. 'The Social Life of Cultural Value'. *Language & Communication* 23: 231–73.

———. 2007. *Language and Social Relations*. Studies in the Social and Cultural Foundations of Language 24. New York: Cambridge University Press.

al-Akhfaš, Saʿīd b. Maṣada. 1970. كتاب القوافي. Edited by Ḥasan ʿIzzat. Damascus: Wizārat al-ṯaqāfa wa-l-siyāḥa wa-l-iršād al-qawmī. Also accessible online at <https://shamela.ws/book/737>.

al-Farrāʾ, Abū Zakariyya Yaḥyā ibn Ziyād. 1955. معاني القرآن. Edited by A. Y. Najātī and M. A. al-Najjār. Cairo: Dār al-kutub al-miṣriyya. Also accessible online at <https:// shamela.ws/book/23634>.

al-Fāsī, David ben Abraham. 1936–1945. כתאב גׄאמע אלאלפאטׄ או אלאגרון תאליף דוד בן אברהם אלפאסי אלמערוף באבי סלימאן דאוד בן אבראהים אלפאסי. Edited by Solomon Leon Skoss. 2 vols. New Haven, CT: Yale University Press.

al-Ğabūrī 1991—see al-Waššāʾ.

al-Jāḥiẓ, Abū ʿUthmān ʿAmr ibn Baḥr. 1998. كتاب البيان والتبيين. Edited by Abdel-Salam Muhammad Haroun. Cairo: Maktabat al-ḫāniǧī bi-l-qāhira.

———. 2003. الحيوان. Edited by Muḥammad Bāsil ʿUyūn al-Sūd. Cairo: Dār al-kutub al-ʿilmiyya. Also accessible online at <https://shamela.ws/book/23775>.

al-Jawharī, Abū Naṣr Ismāʿīl ibn Ḥammād. 1984. الصحاح. Edited by Aḥmad ʿAbd al-Ghafūr ʿAṭṭār. Beirut: Dār al-ʿilm li-l-malāyīn. Also accessible online at <https://shamela.ws/book/23235>.

al-Jumaḥī, Muḥammad ibn Sallām. 1997. طبقات فحول الشعراء. Edited by Maḥmūd Muḥammad Šākir. Judda: Dār al-madanī.

———. 2001. طبقات فحول الشعراء. Edited by Ṭah Aḥmad Ibrāhīm. Beirut: Dār al-Kutub al-ʿIlmiyya.

al-Kisāʾī, Abū al-Ḥasan ʿAlī ibn Ḥamzah. 1982. كتاب ما تلحن فيه العامة. Edited by Ramaḍān Abdel-Tawāb. Cairo: Maktabat al-ḫānijī bi-l-qāhira.

al-Lughawī, Abū al-Ṭayyib ʿAbd al-Wāḥid ibn ʿAlī. 1974/2009. مراتب النحويين. Edited by Muḥammad Abū al-Faḍl Ibrāhīm. Cairo / Beirut: Dār Nahḍat Miṣr / Al-maktaba al-ʿaṣriyya. Also accessible online at <https://books.rafed.net/m/?type=c_fbook&b_id=2548&>.

al-Makhzūmī and al-Sāmarrāʾī 1989—see ibn Aḥmad.

al-Mawlā et al. 1998—see al-Suyūṭī.

al-Qirqisānī, Yaʿqūb ibn Isḥāq. 1939–1945. كتاب الأنوار والمراقب. Edited by Leon Nemoy. 5 vols. New York: The Alexander Kohut Memorial Foundation.

al-Sūd 2003—see al-Jāḥiẓ.

al-Suyūṭī, Jalāl al-Dīn. 1976. الاقتراح في علم أصول النحو. Edited by Aḥmad Muḥammad Qāsim. Cairo: Maṭbaʿat al-Saʿāda. Also accessible online at <https://ar.lib.eshia.ir/10497/1/56>.

al-Suyūṭī, Jalāl al-Dīn. 1989. الإصباح في شرح الاقتراح. Edited by Maḥmūd Fajāl. Cairo: Dār al-Qāhira lil-ṭibāʿa wa-l-našr wal-tawzīʿ.

al-Suyūṭī, Jalāl al-Dīn. 1998. المزهر في علوم اللغة وأنواعها. Edited by Muḥammad Jād al-Mawlā, Muḥammad Abū al-Faḍl Ibrāhīm, and ʿAlī Muḥammad al-Bajjāwī. Cairo: Al-Maktaba al-ʿaṣriyya.

al-Waššāʾ, Muḥammad b. Aḥmad Abū al-Ṭayyib. 1991. كتاب الفاضل في صفة الأدب الكامل. Edited by Yaḥyā Wahīb al-Ğabūrī. Beirut: Dār al-gharb al-islāmī

al-Zubaydī, Abū Bakr Muḥammad ibn al-Ḥasan. 1973. طبقات النحويين واللغويين. Edited by Muḥammad Abū al-Faḍl Ibrāhīm. Cairo: Dār al-Maʿārif.

al-ʿAzzāwī, Niʿma. 1978. النقد اللغوي عند العرب حتى نهاية القرن السابع. Baghdad: Wazārat al-Thaqāfa wa-l-Funūn.

Allony, Nehemiah. 1970. ‘עלי בן יהודה הנזיר וחיבורו "יסודות הלשון העברית"’. *Leshonenu* 34: 75–105, 187.

Alqarni, Hussain M A. 2014. ‘Negotiating Abbasid Modernity: The Case of al-Aṣmaʿī and the Rearguard Poets’. PhD thesis, University of Manchester.

ʿAṭṭār 1984—see al-Jawharī.

Baalbaki, Ramzi. 2008. *The Legacy of the Kitāb: Sībawayhi’s Analytical Methods within the Context of the Arabic Grammatical*

Theory. Studies in Semitic Languages and Linguistics 51. Boston: Brill.

Baer, Seligmann, and Hermann Leberecht Strack. 1879. *Die Dikduke Ha-Teamim des Ahron ben Moscheh ben Ascher und andere alte grammatisch-massoretische Lehrstrücke*. Leipzig: L. Pernoy.

Basal, Nasir. 1998. ‘החלק הראשון של ”אלכתאב אלמשתמל“ לאבו אלפרג׳ הרון ותלותו ב”כתאב אלאצול פי אלנחו“ לאבן אלסראג׳’. *Leshonenu* 61: 191–209.

———. 1999. ‘The Concept of Ḥāl in the Al-Kitāb Al-Mushtamil of Abū Al-Farağ Harūn in Comparison with Ibn Al-Sarrāğ’. In *Compilation and Creation in Adab and Luġa: Studies in Memory of Naphtali Kinberg (1948–1997)*, edited by Albert Arazi, Joseph Sadan, and David J. Wasserstein, 391–408. Israel Oriental Studies 19. Winona Lake, IN: Eisenbrauns.

Bauman, Richard. 1975. ‘Verbal Art as Performance’. *American Anthropologist* 77 (2): 290–311.

Becker, Dan. 1984. ה׳רסאלה׳ של יהודה בן קוריש. Tel-Aviv: Tel-Aviv University.

———. 1998. מקורות ערביים לדקדוקו של ר׳ יונה אבן ג׳נאח. Tel-Aviv: Tel-Aviv University.

———. 2005. מקורות ערביים של ׳ספר ההשוואה בין העברית והערבית׳ ליצחק בן ברון. Tel-Aviv: Tel-Aviv University.

———. 2013. ‘Grammatical Thought, Influence of the Medieval Arabic Grammatical Tradition’. In *Encyclopedia of Hebrew Language and Linguistics*, edited by Geoffrey Khan, II:113–28. Leiden: Brill.

Bell, Allan, and Andy Gibson. 2011. ‘Staging Language: An Introduction to the Sociolinguistics of Performance’. *Journal of Sociolinguistics* 15 (5): 555–72.

ben Labraṭ, Dunaš Ha-Levi. 1866. ספר תשובות דונש הלוי בן לברט על רבי סעדיה גאון. Edited by Robert Schröter. Breslau: Schletter’sche Buchhandlung.

Blachère, R. 1950. ‘Les savants iraquiens et leur informateurs bédouins aux IIe-IVe siècles de l’hégire’. In *Mélanges William Marçais*, 37–48. Paris: G.-P. Maisonneuve.

Blau, Joshua. 1962. ‘על מעמדן של העברית והערבית בין יהודים דוברי ערבית במאות הראשונות של האסלאם’, review of סדרי חינוך בימי הגאונים ובימי הרמב״ם: מקורות חדשים מן הגניזה by Shlomo Dov Goitein. *Leshonenu* 26: 281–84.

———. 1981. *The Renaissance of Modern Hebrew and Modern Standard Arabic: Parallels and Differences in the Revival of Two Semitic Languages*. University of California Publications Near Eastern Studies 18. Berkeley, CA: University of California Press.

———. 2006. *Dictionary of Medieval Judaeo-Arabic Texts*. Jerusalem: Academy of the Hebrew Language.

Bodenheimer, Levi. 1856. *Das Lied Mosis: Eine wissenschaftliche Vergelichung*. Crefeld: Selbstverlage des Verfassers.

Brustad, Kristen. 2010. ‘The Story of the ʿArabiyya, or How the Abbasids Got a Standard Language Ideology’. Paper presented at School of Abbasid Studies Biannual Conference, Catholic University Leuven, 8 July 2010.

———. 2016. ‘The Iconic Sībawayh’. In *Essays in Islamic Philology, History and Philosophy*, edited by Alireza Korangy,

Wheeler M. Thackston, Roy P. Mottahedeh, and William Granara, 141–65. Studies in the History and Culture of the Middle East 31. Berlin: De Gruyter.

———. 2017. 'Diglossia as Ideology'. In *The Politics of Written Language in the Arab World: Writing Change*, edited by Jacob Høigilt and Gunvor Mejdell, 41–67. Studies in Semitic Languages and Linguistics 90. Leiden: Brill.

Carter, M.G. 2004. *Sibawayhi*. London: I. B. Tauris.

Cavanaugh, Jillian R. 2020. 'Language Ideology Revisited'. *International Journal of the Sociology of Language* 263: 51–57.

Derenbourg, Joseph. 1886. *Le livre des parterres fleuries: Grammatique hébraïque en arabe d'Abou'l-Walid Merwan ibn Djanah de Cordoue*. Bibliothèque de l'école des hautes études 66. Paris: F. Vieweg.

———. 1896. *Version Arabe d'Isaïe de R. Saadia ben Iosef al-Fayyoûmî*. Paris: Leroux.

Drory, Rina. 1988. *The Emergence of Jewish-Arabic Literary Contacts at the Beginning of the Tenth Century*. Tel-Aviv: ha-Kibbutz ha-meuḥad. [Hebrew].

———. 1991. 'The Hidden Context: on Literary Products of Tricultural Contacts in the Middle Ages'. *Peʿamim (Studies in Oriental Jewery)* 46–47: 277–302.

———. 2000. *Models and Contacts: Arabic Literature and its Impact on Medieval Jewish Culture*. Brill's Series in Jewish Studies 25. Leiden: Brill.

Fajāl 1989—see al-Suyūṭī.

Fatlī 1996—see ibn al-Sarrāj.

Ferguson, Charles. 1959. 'Diglossia'. *Word* 15: 325–40.

Fleischer, Ezra. 2007. שירת־הקודש העברית בימי־הביניים. Jerusalem: Magnes.

Goitein, Shlomo Dov. 1962. סדרי חינוך בימי הגאונים ובימי הרמב"ם: מקורות חדשים מן הגניזה. Jerusalem: Ben-Zvi Institute.

Gouttenoire, Marie-Andrée. 2006. 'Les Enjeux de l'écriture biographique relative aux savants iraqiens du II/VIIe siècle et à leur transmission du fond Arabo-bédouin'. *Bulletin D'études Orientales* 57: 43–76.

Harkavy, Zvi. 1891. זכרון לראשונים: השריד והפליט מספר האגרון וספר הגלוי. St Petersburg: Ḥevrat Meḳitsei Nirdamim.

Haroun 1988—see Sībawayh.

Haroun 1998—see al-Jāḥiẓ.

Ḥayyūj, Judah ben David. 1897. 'كتاب الأفعال ذوات حروف اللين'. In *The Weak and Geminate Verbs in Hebrew by Abû Zakkariyyâ Yaḥyâ ibn Dâwud of Fez known as Ḥayyûğ*, edited by Morris Jastrow, 1–219. Leiden: Brill.

ibn Aḥmad, al-Khalīl. 1989. كتاب العين. Edited by Mahdī al-Makhzūmī and Ibrāhīm al-Sāmarrā'ī. Beirut: Dār wa-maktabat al-hilāl. Also accessible online at <https://shamela.ws/book/1682>.

ibn al-Sarrāj, Abū Bakr Muḥammad ibn al-Sarī. 1996. كتاب الأصول في النحو. Edited by ʿAbd al-Ḥusayn Fatlī. Beirut: Al-Resalah Publishing House.

ibn Bashkuwal, Abū al-Qāsim. 1955. الصلة في تاريخ أئمة الأندلس. Edited by Baššār ʿAwād Maʿrūf. Cairo: Maktabat al-ḫānijī bi-l-qāhira. Also accessible online at <https://shamela.ws/book/22788>.

ibn Janāḥ, Abū al-Walīd Marwān. 1968. كتاب الأصول لأبى الوليد مروان بن جناح القرطبى ويتلوه منتخبات من تصانيف اخر فى الأصول لبعض علماء المشرق والمغرب. Edited by Adolf Neubauer, with additions and corrections by Wilhelm Bacher. Amsterdam: Philo Press.

Ibrahim, Muhammad H. 1986. 'Standard and Prestige Language: A Problem in Arabic Sociolinguistics'. *Anthropological Linguistics* 28 (1): 115–26.

Ibrāhīm 1973—see al-Zubaydī.

Ibrāhīm 1974/2009—see al-Lughawī.

Ibrāhīm 2001—see al-Jumaḥī.

ʿIzzat 1970—see al-Akhfaš.

Jastrow 1897—see Ḥayyūj.

Johnstone, Barbara. 2016. 'Enregisterment: How Linguistic Items Become Linked with Ways of Speaking'. *Language and Linguistics Compass* 10 (11): 632–43.

Khan, Geoffrey. 1990. 'Al-Qirqisānī's Opinions Concerning the Text of the Bible and Parallel Muslim Attitudes towards the Text of the Qurʾān'. *The Jewish Quarterly Review* 81 (1–2): 59–73.

———. 1998. 'דעות אלקרקסאני על טקסט המקרא ועמדות מוסלמיות מקבילות כלפי טקסט הקוראן'. *Teuda* 14: 69–80.

———. 2013. *A Short Introduction to the Tiberian Masoretic Bible and its Reading Tradition*. Piscataway, NJ: Gorgias.

———. 2020. *The Tiberian Pronunciation Tradition of Biblical Hebrew*. 2 vols. Cambridge Semitic Languages and Cultures 1. Cambridge: Open Book Publishers.

Khan, Geoffrey, María Ángeles Gallego, and Judith Olszowy-Schlanger. 2003. *The Karaite Tradition of Hebrew Grammatical Thought in Its Classical Form: A Critical Edition and English Translation of* al-Kitāb al-Kāfī fī al-Luġa al-ʿIbrāniyya *by ʾAbū al-Faraj Hārūn ibn al-Faraj*. Leiden: Brill.

Khan, Geoffrey, and Benjamin Kantor. 2022. '*Waw* to *Vav*: Greek and Aramaic Contact as an Explanation for the Development of the Labio-Dental [v] from the Labio-velar [w] in Biblical Hebrew'. *Zeitschrift der Deutschen Morgenländischen Gesellschaft* 172 (1): 27–55.

Kokin, D. S. 2013. 'Polemical Discourse'. In *Encyclopedia of Hebrew Language and Linguistics*, edited by Geoffrey Khan, III: 164–69. Leiden: Brill.

Kroskrity, Paul V. (ed.). 2000. *Regimes of Language: Ideologies, Politics, and Identities*. Santa Fe, NM: School of American Research Press.

Lane, Edward William. 1863–1893. *An Arabic-English Lexicon*. 8 vols. London: Williams and Norgate.

Malter, Henry. 1913. 'Saadia Studies: Another Fragment of Saadia's *Sefer Ha-Galui* (Liber Exsulis)'. *Jewish Quarterly Review* 3 (4): 487–509.

———. 1921. *Saadia Gaon: His Life and Works*. Philadelphia: The Jewish Publication Society of America.

Maman, Aharon. 2010. 'Ibn Quraysh, Judah'. In *Encyclopedia of Jews in the Islamic World*, edited by Norman A. Stillman. Leiden: Brill. doi.org/10.1163/1878-9781_ejiw_SIM_0011020.

———. 2004. *Comparative Semitic Philology in the Middle Ages: from Saʿadiah Gaon to Ibn Barūn (10th–12th c.)*. Studies in Semitic Languages and Linguistics 40. Leiden: Brill.

Marogy, Amal. 2010a. 'Kitāb Sībawayhi and Modern Linguistics: A Synoptic View of a Complementary Relationship'. *Synergies Monde arabe* 7: 29–34.

———. 2010b. *Kitāb Sībawayhi: Syntax and Pragmatics*. Studies in Semitic Languages and Linguistics 56. Leiden: Brill.

Maʿrūf 1955—see ibn Bashkuwal.

Milroy, James. 1999. 'The Consequences of Standardisation in Descriptive Linguistics'. In *Standard English: The Widening Debate*, edited by Tony Bex and Richard J. Watts, 16–39. London: Routledge.

———. 2001. 'Language Ideologies and the Consequences of Standardization'. *Journal of Sociolinguistics* 5 (4): 530–55.

Milroy, James, and Lesley Milroy. 1999. *Authority in Language: Investigating Standard English*. London: Routledge.

Morag, Shelomo. 1958. 'A Special Type of Evolution'. In *Proceedings of the VIII International Congress of Linguistics*, edited by Eva Silvertsen, 425–28. Oslo: Oslo University Press.

Najātī and al-Najjār 1955—see al-Farrāʾ.

Nemoy 1939–1945—see al-Qirqisānī.

Neubauer 1968—see ibn Janāḥ.

Pellat, Charles. 2012. 'Laḥn al-ʿāmma'. In *Encyclopaedia of Islam*, edited by P. Bearman, Th. Rianquis, C. E. Bosworth, E. van Donzel, and W. P. Heinrichs, 609–14. 2nd ed. Leiden: Brill.

Qāsim 1976—see al-Suyūṭī.

Rabin, Chaim, Glenda M. Abramson, and Samuel Leiter. Last modified 8 September 2022. 'Hebrew Literature'. In *Encyclopedia Britannica Online*. https://www.britannica.com/art/Hebrew-literature.

Rand, Michael. 2013. 'Paytanic Hebrew'. In *Encyclopedia of Hebrew Language and Linguistics*, edited by Geoffrey Khan, III: 55–60. Leiden: Brill.

———. 2014. *Introduction to the Grammar of Hebrew Poetry in Byzantine Palestine*. Gorgias Studies in Language and Linguistics 22. Piscataway, NJ: Gorgias.

Sáenz-Badillos, Angel. 2013. 'Medieval Hebrew'. In *Encyclopedia of Hebrew Language and Linguistics*, edited by Geoffrey Khan, II: 624–33. Leiden: Brill.

Šākir 1997—see al-Jumaḥī.

Sasson, Ilana. 2016. 'Ibn Quraysh, Judah'. In *Encyclopedia of the Bible and Its Reception*, edited by Dale C. Allison, Jr., Christine Helmer, Steven L. McKenzie, Thomas Römer, Jens Schröter, Choon Leong Seow, Barry Dov Walfish, and Eric J. Ziolkowski, XII: 749–50. Berlin: De Gruyter.

Schechter, Solomon. 1903. *Saadyana: Geniza Fragments of Writings of R. Saadya Gaon and Others*. Cambridge: Deighton and Bell.

Schieffelin, Bambi B., Kathryn A. Woolard, and Paul V. Kroskrity (eds). 1998. *Language Ideologies: Practice and Theory*. New York: Oxford University Press.

Shivtiel, Avihai. 2007. Review of *Arabic Sources of Isaac ben Barūn's Book of Comparison between the Hebrew and the Arabic Language*, by Dan Becker. *Journal of Semitic Studies* 52 (2): 397–99.

Schröter 1866—see ben Labraṭ.

Sībawayh. 1988. الكتاب. Edited by Abdel-Salam Muhammad Haroun. Cairo: Maktabat al-ẖānijī bi-l-qāhira. Also accessible online at <https://shamela.ws/book/23018>.

Silverstein, Michael. 1993. 'Metapragmatic Discourse and Metapragmatic Function'. In *Reflexive Language: Reported Speech and Metapragmatics*, edited by John A. Lucy, 33–58. Cambridge: Cambridge University Press.

———. 2003. 'Indexical Order and the Dialectics of Sociolinguistic Life'. *Language and Communication* 23: 193–229.

———. 1952a. 'A Study of Hebrew Vowels from Saadia Gaon's Grammatical Work "Kutub al-Lughah"'. *Jewish Quarterly Review* 42: 283–317.

———. 1952b. 'Saadia Gaon: The Earliest Hebrew Grammarian'. *Proceedings of the American Academy for Jewish Research* 21: 75–100.

Skoss 1936–1945—see al-Fāsī.

Stokes, Phillip. 2017. 'A Historical Grammar of Case in Arabic'. PhD dissertation, University of Texas at Austin.

Suleiman, Yasir. 1999. *The Arabic Grammatical Tradition: A Study in Taʿlīl*. Edinburgh: Edinburgh University Press.

———. 2003. *The Arabic Language and National Identity*. Edinburgh: Edinburgh University Press.

———. 2011. 'Ideology, Grammar-Making and the Standardization of Arabic'. In *In the Shadow of Arabic: The Centrality of Language to Arabic Culture*, edited by Bilal Orfali, 3–30. Studies in Semitic Languages and Linguistics 63. Leiden: Brill.

Talmon, Rafael. 2003. *Eighth-Century Iraqi Grammar: A Critical Exploration of Pre-Khalīlian Arabic Linguistics*. Cambridge, MA: Harvard Semitic Museum Publications.

Tobi, Yosef. 2004. *Proximity and Distance: Medieval Hebrew and Arabic Poetry*. Études sur le judaïsme médiéval 27. Leiden: Brill.

Touati, Houari. 2010. *Islam & Travel in the Middle Ages*. Chicago: University of Chicago Press.

van Gelder, Geert Jan. 1997. 'Dubious Genres: On Some Poems by Abū Nuwās'. *Arabica* 44 (2): 268–83.

van Putten, Marijn. 2022. *Quranic Arabic: From its Hijazi Origins to its Classical Reading Traditions*. Leiden: Brill.

Wahba, Kassem M. 2023. 'A Historical Overview of Arabic Grammar Instruction'. In *Teaching and Learning Arabic Grammar: Theory, Practice, and Research*, edited by Kassem M. Wahba, Zeinab Taha, and Manuela Giolfo. New York: Routledge. doi.org/10.4324/9781003034209-2.

Webb, Peter. 2016. *Imagining the Arabs: Arab Identity and the Rise of Islam*. Edinburgh: Edinburgh University Press.

Woolard, Kathryn A. 1998. 'Introduction: Language Ideology as a Field of Inquiry'. In *Language Ideologies: Practice and Theory*, edited by Bambi B. Schieffelin, Kathryn A. Woolard, and Paul V. Kroskrity, 3–50. Oxford: Oxford University Press.

Woolard, Kathryn A. and Bambi B. Schieffelin. 1994. 'Language Ideology'. *Annual Review of Anthropology* 23 (1):55–82.

Ya'akov, Doron. 2015. מסורת העברית שבפי יהודי דרום תימן: מערכת ההגה ולשון המשנה. Jerusalem: Magnes.

Yahalom, Joseph, and Naoya Katsumata. 2014. יוצרות רבי שמואל השלישי: מראשי ההנהגה בירושלים במאה העשירית. Vol. 1. Jerusalem: Yad Izhak Ben-Zvi.

INDEX

A

ʿAbbasid, 3, 41–42, 53, 62, 177, 179, 184

accent, 28–29

accusative, 67, 82, 142, 171

action, 19, 69, 145

adjectives, 11, 63–65, 113, 124

agent, 48, 52, 142, 147

al-Awsaṭ, al-Akhfaš, 96

al-Azharī, 99, 172

al-Aʿša, 63–65

al-Duʾalī, Abū al-Aswad, 141–142, 147, 168–171, 174

al-Fārābī, Abū Naṣr, 142, 166, 168, 174–175

al-Farrāʾ, Abū Zakariyya Yaḥyā ibn Ziyād, 7, 9, 51–52, 72, 77–79, 100, 114, 150

al-Fasī, David ben Abraham, 57, 92, 126, 136, 138, 140, 150, 174

al-Ḫaṭṭāb, Abū, 68

al-Jāḥiẓ, Abū ʿUthmān ʿAmr ibn Baḥr, 143–144, 147, 164–166, 174–175

al-Jarrāḥ, Abū, 100

al-Jawharī, Abū Naṣr Ismāʿīl ibn Ḥammād, 99, 101

al-Jumaḥī, ibn Sallām, 79–81, 114, 141–143, 146, 168–169, 171, 175

al-Kisāʾī, Abū al-Ḥasan ʿAlī ibn Ḥamzah, 100, 145

al-Lughawī, Abū al-Ṭayyib, 168–169, 174–175

al-Mirbad, 97

al-Mubarrad, 7, 83

al-Nahāwandī, Benjamin, 113

al-Najūd, ʿĀṣim ibn Abī, 170

al-Qirqisānī, Jacob, 9, 149, 157, 159, 161–163, 168, 174–176, 185

al-Waššāʾ, Muḥammad b. Aḥmad Abū al-Ṭayyib, 99

al-Zubaydī, Abū Bakr Muḥammad ibn al-Ḥasan, 100–101, 142, 170–171, 175

al-ʿAṣmaʿī, 102

al-ʿAttābī, 165

Algerian, 161

Amman, 29

ʿāmmiyya, 22

Ammonite, 155–156

analogy, 27, 133–135, 141, 165, 180, 183, 185

ancestors, 86, 147, 156, 161–162
ancient, 4, 7, 10, 13, 15–16, 27, 33, 35, 54–57, 59–60, 62–63, 74–75, 83–87, 89, 105–106, 108–110, 122, 128, 136, 175, 177–178
ancients, 56, 69, 79, 110, 162
Andalus, 45–46, 81, 100, 133
Arabia, 71, 106, 144
Arabic, Classical, 12, 14, 38, 61, 76, 181, 183
Arabic, Egyptian, 117
Arabic, Jordanian, 28
Arabic, Judeo-, 3, 14, 41, 45, 90, 120, 177, 179
Arabic, Modern Standard, 13, 38
ʿarabiyya, 6–7, 15, 43, 64, 67–70, 80, 87–89, 96–97, 101, 103, 107, 113–115, 117, 141–142, 169–171, 182
Arabs/Arabness, 6, 10, 12–13, 38, 43, 49–54, 62–66, 68–69, 71, 73–86, 101, 103, 113–116, 141–143, 145–146, 150, 158, 165–166, 168–174, 177, 179–180, 182
Aramaic, 12, 91–92, 149, 152–154, 156, 158–159, 161–164, 167, 173, 176, 181
archaic, 35
artefacts, textual, 33, 129
Ashdodite, 155–156
attitude towards foreign languages, 23, 149, 174, 177, 183
  negative, 4, 23, 65, 148–149, 163, 168, 174–175, 177–178, 183
  positive, 149, 163, 176
audience, 31, 35–36, 66, 70, 87, 108
authority, 9–10, 23, 25–26, 64, 70–71, 101, 106, 128, 136–138, 146, 161, 175

B

Babylon, 9, 154, 156, 185
Baghdad, 52, 99–100
Bahrain, 167
Banū Asad, 68
Banū Ḥanīfa, 167
Banū Tamīm, 68
Baṣra, 10, 49, 80, 97, 170
Baṣrans, 116, 141, 168
Bedouin, 14, 83, 89, 96–108, 144, 166, 168, 178, 181
Bedouinisation, 103

beginner, 81–82
ben Barūn, Isaac, 6–8
ben Labraṭ, Dunaš, 124, 126
ben Saruq, Menaḥem, 133–134
ben Zakkai, David, 126
Berber, 163
Bible, 1–2, 7–11, 13–16, 45–48, 55–60, 62, 85–86, 91, 93, 95–96, 102, 107–110, 112, 120, 122, 124–125, 128–135, 147, 149, 153, 155–159, 162–164, 168, 176, 180–182, 185
binyanim, 1
borrowing, 15
Boston, 28
boundary, 98
branch, 56, 80–81, 168
Byzantine, 55, 60–61, 86, 159–160, 165

C
Cairo, 6
calques, 7
canon, 14, 16, 23–27, 32, 35, 53, 55, 61, 85–86, 108, 117, 138, 140, 148, 174, 179
case system, 44, 62, 64–65, 69, 74–76, 79, 89, 119–120, 132, 143, 147, 169–171
catalyst, 118, 131, 148
categorisation, 71–72, 74, 80, 146
children, 102, 133, 155–156, 165, 170
Christians, 167
chronology, 32–33, 60, 75, 83, 87, 104, 141, 175
circulation, 26, 30–32, 37, 118
class, 29, 144
classification, 80
climate, 95, 106
Cockney, 28–29
codes, 35
codicology, 129, 148
codification, 3, 11, 20, 25–26, 40, 75, 79, 83, 118, 134, 136, 141–143, 168, 170, 174
cognitive, 22
colloquial speech, 14, 21, 26, 28, 35, 62, 65, 72–74, 91–92, 99, 110–114, 117, 138, 163, 182
commonfolk, 90–92, 95, 102, 178, 181
communication, 14, 22, 33, 36, 94, 112–113, 128, 166
communities, 1, 9, 12–14, 16, 19–21, 23, 37, 40, 43, 49, 62, 73, 76–77, 83, 86, 93, 95–96, 103, 106, 112, 114,

120–121, 123, 130, 138, 140, 146–147, 153, 156–159, 168, 172
Comparative Semitics, 10, 161
complaint tradition, 23–25, 30, 109, 113, 115, 117–118, 131, 134–136, 138, 140, 143–144, 146–149, 153, 155–157, 159, 161–162, 164, 166, 168–171, 173–175, 177–179, 183
composition, 3, 12, 44, 109–110, 116, 118–122, 124, 129–130, 132, 135–136, 139–140, 142, 146, 148, 169–170, 173, 181
conjugation, 111, 131–132, 134–135, 142, 180
conjunctions, 48, 53
connotation, 35, 62, 73, 83, 103, 125, 143, 173
conquest, 143, 146, 156, 169–171
consonants, 9, 46, 57, 68, 72, 76, 124, 133–135
contemporary, 4, 6, 15, 35, 42, 53–56, 59, 67, 69, 72–74, 84–86, 88–90, 96, 102, 104, 106, 108, 112, 117, 126, 132, 140, 148–149, 156, 168, 174–177, 182, 185
conventions, 45, 81, 122
conversation, 21, 28, 31, 35, 74, 99, 102, 113
Copts, 167
corpus, 3–4, 14, 27, 33, 40–41, 55, 59, 62–66, 69, 71, 73, 75, 81–82, 84–89, 108, 113–114, 142, 153, 177–178, 181, 185
correctness, 7, 22, 24, 27, 29, 44, 55, 57–59, 61–63, 78, 83–84, 97, 101, 105, 111–112, 117, 119–120, 126, 128–129, 132–136, 140, 144–147, 158, 160–161, 177, 180
corruption, 14, 24, 98, 118, 130, 132, 135, 140, 161, 164–166, 168–169, 174
criteria, 9, 36, 40, 61, 76
cultural possession, 3, 22–23, 25, 43–44, 53, 85–86, 104, 128, 148, 153, 163, 176–177, 179
culture, 3–4, 6, 12–15, 19, 21–27, 30–32, 35, 37, 40, 42–44, 53–54, 62, 71, 77, 83, 85–86, 97, 103–104, 106, 108, 116–117, 128, 144, 148, 153, 163, 169, 173–174, 176–180, 182–185

customs, 22

D

declension, 120
declivity, 111, 131–132, 169, 171
definiteness, 68–69, 113
degeneracy, 26, 175
delegitimisation, 158, 174
demographics, 34, 94–96, 104–107, 178, 181
derivation, 60, 73, 81–82, 127, 132, 136, 164, 180
descendants, 160
desert, 15, 83, 89, 96–99, 101–107, 144, 166, 168, 178, 181
diachrony, 172
dialects, 22, 26, 38, 69, 72–74, 76, 114, 141, 143
Diaspora, 61, 158–159
diction, 136
diglossia, 14, 21–22
diversity, 20, 22, 26, 64, 66, 76, 82, 86, 88, 114, 181, 184–185
documentation, 1, 63, 70, 74, 76, 88, 105, 116–118

E

ʿEber, 44, 154
economy, 19, 97
education, 5–6, 16, 29, 112, 184
elision, 50
eloquence/*faṣāḥa*, 6, 11, 23, 38, 45, 64–65, 92–94, 96, 98–99, 110, 119–132, 136, 143–144, 147, 149–154, 156–157, 164–166, 172–174, 178, 180, 183
emergence of grammar, 4, 82, 141–142, 146, 173, 178, 180, 183
enclitics, 50
English, 21, 28, 30, 42, 126
enregisterment, 20, 27–34, 61, 69, 87, 93–96, 107, 129, 136, 148, 178
Ethiopians, 167
ethnic, 23, 29–30, 62, 65, 71, 73, 77, 83, 103, 106, 172–173, 178
etymology, 164
Europe, 22
evolution, 1, 73, 83, 88, 103
exemplary speakers, 4, 31, 54–55, 58, 60, 62, 68–69, 85–87, 89–90, 92, 104–106, 108, 177–178, 180
Exilarch, 126
exile, 126, 154, 156, 160

experts in the language, 70, 80–81, 165

F
Fayyūm/Upper Egypt, 43
fieldwork, 4, 15–16, 55, 89–91, 96, 99, 102–105, 144, 177–178, 181
foreigners, 4, 23, 125, 148–153, 155–157, 159, 161, 163–166, 168–178, 183
forgetting the language, 44, 118–121, 130, 146–148, 151–153, 155–157
fuṣḥā, 22, 63

G
Galilee, 89
Gaon, Saadia, 11, 14–16, 43–44, 53, 58–62, 87–89, 109–112, 115, 118–132, 137–138, 140, 146–147, 149–157, 161, 173, 175–176, 180, 183
Gaonate, 126
genealogists, 71
Genizah, 6
genre, 2, 5, 12–13, 32, 60, 114–116, 144–147
geography, 83, 93–99, 104–107, 160, 176, 181
Ghassān, 167
gibberish, 165–166
gizzɔ̄rōn, 164
grammar, 1–5, 8, 11, 20, 24–26, 40, 43, 46–47, 50, 76–77, 81–84, 87–88, 101, 114, 116, 118, 120, 122–123, 125–126, 130–131, 137, 141–143, 148–149, 169, 171, 173–174, 178–180, 183–184
grammaticality, 9, 109, 122
Greek, 60, 151, 159, 161, 167
Greeks, 155

H
ha-Nazir, ʿEli ben Yehudah, 15, 90, 92, 102, 106, 181
hadith, 81
hamzah, 45, 50
handbook, 32
Ḥanīfa, Abū, 7
hašvɔ̄ʾɔ̄, 164
Ḥayyūj, Judah ben David, 180, 182, 185
hearers, 28–29, 92, 96, 143, 165, 180
Hebrew, Biblical, 1–2, 9, 16, 45–48, 57, 86, 120, 130, 134, 149, 153, 158–159,

162–164, 168, 180–182, 185
Hebrew, Payṭanic, 181–182
Hebrew, Rabbinic, 85–86, 180, 182
Hebrews, 10, 42–48, 54–57, 85, 89, 94, 112, 119–120, 123–126, 130, 136, 177
heirs, 106
heritage, 4, 22, 93, 115
Ḥijāz, 10, 158, 168
Ḥijāzī, 72–73
Ḥimyar, 114
historicisation, 26, 88, 106, 174–175, 177
historicity, 72
homographic, 146

I

ibn Aḥmad, al-Khalīl, 62, 116
ibn al-Faraj, Abū al-Faraj Hārūn, 6–8, 47–48, 95, 106
ibn al-Jinnī, 99
ibn al-Sarrāj, Abū Bakr Muḥammad ibn al-Sarī, 7–8, 52, 81–84, 88
ibn al-Sikkīt, 146
ibn Barmark, Yaḥyā ibn Khālid, 100
ibn Bashkuwal, Abū al-Qāsim, 81
ibn Durayd, 99
ibn Janāḥ, Jonah/Abū al-Walīd Marwān, 6
ibn Qurayš, Yehudah, 149, 161–163, 176
ibn Qutayba, 71
ibn Yaḥyā, Abū al-ʿAbbās Aḥmad, 122, 183
iḍāfa, 69, 142
idealised language, 20–22, 24, 55, 69, 83, 85, 98, 129
identity, 23, 28, 54, 89, 153, 161, 174
ideological construct, 21–22, 89, 92, 96
idioms, 63
ijmāʿ, 9
illǧīm, 150–151
imitation, 6, 15, 26, 57, 59, 82, 85, 128–130, 180–181
incorrectness, 24, 27, 29–30, 111, 117, 132, 134, 145, 147
indefinite, 76
indexicality, 27, 95
Indians, 167
infinitive, 132–133
influence, 3–4, 8, 18, 23, 26, 40, 77, 102, 150, 153, 159, 161, 163–164, 168, 174–176, 178–181, 183–184

informal, 21
informants, 4, 14, 71, 89, 96–97, 101–102, 181
inhabitants, 15, 90, 161, 167, 182
inheritance, 2, 106, 122, 154, 185–186
institutionalisation, 25–26, 70, 87–88, 135, 148
institutions, 112
intelligibility, 24, 38, 147
interface, Hebrew-Arabic, 2–3, 5–6, 8, 13–16, 18
intermarriage, 155–156
intermingling, 165–167, 170–171, 174
Iraq, 101, 158–160
Iraqis, 160
Isaiah, 120, 124–126, 149–152, 157
Iṣfahān, 158
Ishmaelites, 121
Islam, 62–67, 69, 71–72, 74–76, 80, 84, 86, 104, 146, 156, 166, 169–171, 181
Israel, 160–161, 168
Israelites, 43, 122, 160

J
Jacob's blessing, 92
Jāhiliyyah, 63, 65, 80
jazm, 142
Jaʿfar, 97
Jerusalem, 47
Jewish, 5–6, 12–16, 37, 93, 95–96, 112, 123, 151–154, 156–157, 163, 179–180
Judahite, 155
Judaism, 14
Juḏām, 167

K
kalām al-ʿibrānī, 152, 156
kalām al-ʿarab, 10, 43, 49–52, 54, 62–66, 69, 71, 73, 75–86, 103, 113–116, 142–143, 145–146, 165, 169–170, 182
Karaites, 14, 47, 57, 112, 138, 157
Kūfa, 10
Kūfans, 51, 168

L
laḥn al-ʿāmma, 144–147
lām sākina, 78
language learning, 6, 12, 39, 53, 56, 82, 120, 127–128, 130, 143, 146, 156, 177
language use, 4, 12, 14, 19, 21–22, 24, 26, 47–51, 53, 64, 69, 91, 109–111, 115,

118, 120, 131–132, 137–138, 146–147, 177
language varieties, 21, 27, 30, 32, 34, 72, 74, 168, 175
Latin, 22, 151
leaders, 142–143, 147
lectures, 21
legacy, 1, 185–186
legitimisation, 25–26, 57–58, 88, 158
letters, 45–46, 49, 55, 57–58, 101, 111, 116, 131–132, 134–135, 142
Levantine, 158
Levites, 154
lexica, 8, 25, 38, 49, 57, 92, 101, 115, 126, 136, 139–140, 150, 163, 171, 174
lexicographers, 49, 57, 71, 89, 99, 101, 137, 139–140, 161, 172
lexicography, 163, 172–173, 183
linguistic anthropology, 1–2, 13, 17–19, 27, 32–34, 117, 176
linguistic benefit, 13, 56, 119, 127, 136, 146, 162–163
linguistic decay/ineptitude among the masses, 4, 24–26, 110, 118, 132, 135–136, 140–144, 146–149, 152–153, 156, 162, 164–165, 170–171, 173, 175, 182–183
linguistic environment, 14, 158, 166
linguistic errors, 98, 100, 113, 142–144, 146–147, 159, 166, 169, 171, 174, 180, 182
linguistic evaluation, 7, 20, 36, 56, 59, 61, 66–67, 69–70, 87–89, 100, 105–106, 177–178, 180
linguistic production, 24, 85, 109–110, 182
linguistics, 1–2, 7–8, 12–14, 16–21, 23, 27–37, 39, 45–48, 51–52, 54–57, 61–62, 66, 69, 74–76, 82, 86–87, 89–90, 92–96, 98–101, 103, 105–106, 108, 110–111, 114–118, 121–122, 126, 128–129, 134, 139, 143, 146–148, 153, 157, 166–167, 172–176, 178, 180–183, 185
lisān al-ʿarab/lisān ʿarabī, 10, 113, 168
literacy, 182

literature, 2–3, 5–6, 13–22, 31, 42, 79, 96, 102–103, 118, 130, 163, 181
liturgy, 35, 60, 92, 110, 112, 163, 180–182
loanwords, 23, 164, 185
locales, 28, 106, 166, 182
locus, 102, 104, 144
London, 29
lukna, 143

M

maḏāhib, 157
maintenance, 12, 25–26, 103, 112, 117, 148, 177–178
majority, 7, 9–10, 23–24, 46
malḥūn, 109, 144
malleability, 26
maqāma, 13
marketplace, 110
Masoretes, 90, 93–95, 102, 104–106
Masoretic, 96, 107
masters, 165
mawālī, 169, 174
Mecca, 10
media, 21, 31, 34
medieval, 1–6, 8, 10, 12–15, 18, 32–35, 37, 40–42, 54, 58, 77, 87, 89, 92–93, 112, 125, 177, 185–186
Medina, 10
metadiscourse, 32
metaphor, 35
methodology, 46
methods, 101, 130, 135–137
metrics, 38
Middle Ages, 1–3, 5–6, 10, 15, 18, 37, 39, 43, 93, 111, 159, 177
misconjugation, 132–134, 146–147
Mishnah, 10, 55–56, 60
mission, 108, 120, 122, 131, 151, 183
Moabite, 155–156
models, 14–15, 129–130
modern, 21–22, 27, 33–34, 38, 42, 45, 62, 159, 185
modernisation, 14
moderns, 36, 73, 107, 184
monikers, 165, 177
morality (and language), 23, 127–128
Moroccans, 160
Morocco, 45
morphology, 38, 49, 52, 60, 67, 111, 122, 131–132, 134, 147, 172, 180, 185
Moses, 11
motivation, 16, 19, 118, 124, 131, 136, 146

Muhammad, 11, 144, 169
mursal, 123
Muslim, 5–6, 9, 12–16, 37
mutaʿarribūn, 169

N
Nabatean, 152–153
Nabateanisation, 158
Nabateans, 158–159, 167
Namir, 167
Naphtali, 92
narrative, 92, 154, 168
narrators, 80
nation, 9–10, 44, 109, 119, 121, 123, 129–131, 146, 149, 151–154, 157–158, 164, 167–168, 174, 178
national, 16
native, 23–24, 38, 53, 56, 61, 69, 85, 117, 142, 156, 177
natural, 47, 143
negation, 65–66
neglect, 24, 101, 118, 123, 131–132, 138–140, 146, 152, 162, 173, 178–179, 183
Nehemiah, 155–157, 173
niqqud, 120
nomenclature, 42–43, 45, 49
nominal, 124, 126, 146
nominative, 74, 82, 142, 171
Nuwās, Abū, 97–98

O
oaths, 65
omission, 51–52, 65, 77–78, 113
onomatopoeia, 50
opposite, 59, 151, 172, 174
oppositions, 29, 144, 146–147, 172–173, 183
Oral Historians, 71
orality, 75, 115–116
orations, 110–112, 115–117, 132
orators, 135
orthography, 45, 78, 129

P
Palestine, 60–61, 158, 175
Palestinian, 9, 158–161, 174
Palestinians, 159–160
paradigm, 15, 134
parallelism, 35
participles, 48
particle, 53, 65
patient, 142, 145, 147
pedagogy, 82, 112
Peninsula, 98, 106, 167
perfection, 98, 106
performance/elevated register, 4, 14, 28, 31–38, 62, 65,

69–75, 96, 103, 106, 108–110, 112–117, 123, 128, 131, 134, 142, 146, 153, 177–178, 182–183
permissibility, 26, 48–49, 51, 58, 66, 74, 157–158, 170
Persian, 50, 74, 101, 150, 159
Persians, 159, 167
Peshitta, 151
philologists, 73, 76–77, 84, 97–101, 133, 161
philology, 10, 159, 161
philosopher, 166
phonology, 28, 38, 159, 161, 163
phraseology, 87–88, 115
piyyuṭ, 15, 55, 60–62, 86, 110, 134, 180–182, 185
  payṭanim, 15, 55, 60, 62, 110, 180
    ben Qalir, Eleazar, 59–61, 180
    Phinehas the Priest, 59–60, 180
    Yannai, 59–61, 180
    Yehoshua, 59–60, 180
    Yose ben Yose, 59–60, 180
pleasing, 59, 61, 68–70, 75, 87, 106, 180
poetry, 7, 12, 15, 21, 36, 50, 52, 55, 58–69, 71–82, 84, 86, 89, 96–100, 102, 104, 109–112, 114–117, 119–120, 122, 128–130, 132, 135, 141, 146–147, 154, 178–182
Poetry Reciters, 71
pointing, 120, 147
political, 1, 19, 23, 25
politics, 18
populace, 91, 105, 181
popular, 31–32, 37
popularisation, 14, 32
population, 12, 24–25, 90, 92–94, 102, 104–108, 179
populations, 169
prefixes, 50, 142
preformative *mem*, 48
prepositions, 142, 145
prescriptivism, 32, 38, 49, 66, 84, 88, 108, 117, 145
preservation, 15, 23, 25, 83, 93, 124, 161
prestige, 15, 21, 26–27, 30–31, 37, 75, 93–96, 105, 117, 163, 181
priests, 60, 154
priority, 73
professional, 128

proficiency, 4, 6, 23, 25, 31, 36, 86, 106–107, 109–110, 115, 138–140, 146–148, 151, 153, 178
pronouns, 28
pronunciation, 15, 28–30, 38, 51–52, 68, 77, 90, 95, 102, 146, 158–159
prooftexts, 63
prophecy, 56–57, 120, 125, 149–151, 157
prophets, 11, 154, 169
prose, 97
proverbs, 63, 115–116, 128, 182
public, 25, 31–32, 36, 110–112, 115, 128
purity, 15, 75, 84, 92, 96, 98–99, 105–106, 125, 166, 173, 178

Q
qirāʾāt, 76
Quḍāʿa, 167
Qurʾān, 7–9, 11, 13–15, 38, 51–52, 62–63, 66–67, 69, 71–78, 81–82, 84–86, 104, 113–114, 116, 181
  Al-Fajr, 51
  Az-Zukhruf, 72
  Luqman, 145
Qurʾān Reading Authorities, 71

R
Rabbanite Judaism, 14
Rabbinic, 85–86, 180, 182
readers, 9–10, 26, 33, 38, 41, 45, 51, 57, 59, 61, 70–71, 82, 87, 128–129, 136, 140, 144, 147–148
Readers who Perform with Melodies, 71
reading, 8–10, 15–16, 46, 57, 71–72, 76–77, 82, 90, 93–96, 119, 124, 130, 146, 149–151, 157–161, 163, 168, 172–175, 185
reading tradition, 9, 15, 90, 93–94, 96, 158–161, 163, 168
realisations, 50, 86, 159
recitations, 11, 36, 52, 68–69, 72, 74, 76, 96–97, 107, 109–110, 112, 114–115, 122, 167, 181
reconstruction, 33, 135
recontextualisation, 83
regional variation, 28–30, 38, 146, 156, 158
registers, 11, 22, 28, 30–33, 37, 62, 65, 71–74, 108, 113–114, 116–117, 126,

129, 142, 148, 177–178, 183
regularisation, 45, 134
regularity, 134
religion, 12–13, 16, 22–23, 37, 73, 112, 163
Renaissance, 13
repatriation, 156
residents, 28–29, 95
residing, 93, 168
restoration, 16, 110, 112, 118, 121, 129, 131, 138, 157, 174–175, 183
rhetoric, 36, 99
rhymes, 35, 96–97, 109, 122, 180
riddles, 139
ridicule, 36
roots, 45–46, 133
rules, 1, 6, 20, 22, 24, 26, 66, 72, 75–76, 81–82, 84, 88, 91, 109–110, 122, 141–142
rural, 97–98, 103

S

sacred, 11, 13–14, 16, 36, 55, 62, 85, 106, 177–179
salīqiyya, 142–143
schools, 25–26, 31
semantics, 77, 83, 103, 120, 126, 146
semivowels, 131
sermons, 36
shewa, 45–46
Shiraz, 50
Sībawayh, 7, 9, 50–51, 62–67, 69–77, 79, 82–89, 100, 103, 113–114, 150, 180
signals, 35
social, 25, 27–34, 61, 87, 93–94, 97, 105, 117, 184
societal, 27, 30–33, 35, 37, 96, 148, 173, 176
societies, 12, 21, 179
society, 12–13, 18–19, 22–24, 27, 30–32, 34, 36–37, 40, 53–54, 61, 75, 85, 103, 108, 179
sociohistorical, 30–32, 39
sociolinguistics, 2–3, 31–32, 39, 104, 117
songs, 154
Spain, 45
Spanish, 21, 42
speakers, 3–4, 10, 18, 21–24, 28–32, 34–36, 38, 42–43, 47, 49, 51, 53–58, 60–62, 67, 69–70, 73–74, 76, 81–83, 85–87, 89–90, 92, 103–108, 117, 134, 143, 146, 166, 170, 172, 177–178, 180

speech, 1, 10, 19, 21, 28, 30–36, 43, 46–54, 56–57, 62–63, 65, 70–71, 73–74, 76–77, 83, 85, 89–94, 98, 103–104, 106, 110–111, 117, 126–128, 130, 136, 138, 142–145, 147, 157, 161, 164–166, 168, 172, 174, 181–182
speeches, 21, 31, 36, 110–112, 115–117, 132, 146–147, 178, 182
stammerers, 120, 124, 149–151
standard language ideology, 3, 20, 22, 29, 35, 41–42, 45, 53–55, 85, 88, 105, 108, 117–118, 128, 140, 144, 147–148, 159, 176–177, 179, 184–185
standardisation, 20–21, 26, 69–70, 79, 83
stutterers, 151
stuttering, 151
style, 35, 60–61, 110, 125, 128–132, 178, 180–183
substandard, 175
suburban, 30
suffixes, 50, 145
syllable, 45–46
synagogue, 112, 182
syntax, 7, 38, 67, 142
Syria, 167
Syriac, 151
systematisation, 134, 185

T

Tafsīr, 150–152
Taghlib, 167
Talmud, 13–14
tanwīn, 50, 64, 67, 69
targets (of enregisterment), 29, 87
Targum, 91, 162
Ṭāʾif, 167
teachers, 31, 133
teaching, 6, 25, 129–130, 140, 152
Temple, 154, 160
temporal, 48, 85
tense, 48
terminology, 7, 10, 38, 125, 183
textualisation, 78
ṭeʿamim/accents, 128–129
Thaqīf, 167
Thaʿlab, 122, 183
Tiberian, 9, 15, 46, 57, 89–90, 92–96, 102, 104–107, 158, 160–161, 174, 185
Tiberians, 15, 94–96, 99, 105–106, 108, 160

Tiberias, 15, 89–95, 99, 102, 105–106, 178, 181
tongues, 60, 102, 120, 124–125, 149–151, 157
topoi, 4, 13–16, 55, 89, 91, 97, 102–104, 144, 177–178, 181
tradents, 69, 94, 161, 168, 174
traditional society, 12–13
transference, 27, 31, 34, 90, 93–95, 106–107, 179
translation, 82, 101, 123–127, 150–152, 162, 166, 185
transliterations, 7
transmission, 9, 30–31, 69, 71, 75, 101, 122, 142, 160–161, 168
treatises, 3, 32, 99, 102, 132, 147–148
tribes, 166, 168
triliteral, 1
trope, 96

U
ʿUmān, 167
ungrammaticality, 100, 144
uniformity, 20, 23, 26, 161, 185
unintelligibility, 110
urban, 14, 29–30, 97–98, 103, 166
urbanisation, 12
users, 24–25, 37–38, 47, 55, 107, 138, 140, 174
-ūṯ ending, 124
ʿUthmānic Text, 9

V
validation, 9, 35
valorisation, 30–31, 37, 118
variation, 20, 38, 49, 70, 72, 76, 114, 120, 137, 146, 175, 185
verbal art, 35
verbal mood, 69, 74–75, 89
verbal morphology, 49, 70, 77–78, 131–132, 135, 185
verbal root, 180
verbs, 52, 111, 131–136, 146–147, 180, 182
vernacular, 22, 92, 111, 156, 159, 161, 163, 174, 181
verses, 50, 52, 63, 77, 97, 99, 120, 124–125, 128, 149–152
vocabulary, 23, 98
vocalisation, 36, 46, 57, 89, 124, 160, 185
vowels, 35, 44, 46, 52, 68, 76, 78, 120, 128
vowels, Arabic, 52, 68
vowels, Hebrew, 159

Vulgate, 151

W
weakness, 111, 131, 140
worship, 157–158

Y
Yamāma, 167
Yemen, 114, 158, 167
Yemenite, 159
Yūnus, 99

Z
Zarqa, 28–29
Ziyād, 170

About the Team

Alessandra Tosi was the managing editor for this book and provided quality control.

Anne Burberry performed the copyediting of the book in Word. The main fonts used in this volume are SIL Charis SIL, SBL Hebrew, and Scheherazade New.

Cameron Craig created all of the editions — paperback, hardback, and PDF. Conversion was performed with open source software freely available on our GitHub page at https://github.com/OpenBookPublishers.

Jeevanjot Kaur Nagpal designed the cover of this book. The cover was produced in InDesign using Fontin and Calibri fonts.

Cambridge Semitic Languages and Cultures

General Editor Geoffrey Khan

OPEN ACCESS

Cambridge Semitic Languages and Cultures

About the series

This series is published by Open Book Publishers in collaboration with the Faculty of Asian and Middle Eastern Studies of the University of Cambridge. The aim of the series is to publish in open-access form monographs in the field of Semitic languages and the cultures associated with speakers of Semitic languages. It is hoped that this will help disseminate research in this field to academic researchers around the world and also open up this research to the communities whose languages and cultures the volumes concern. This series includes philological and linguistic studies of Semitic languages and editions of Semitic texts. Titles in the series will cover all periods, traditions and methodological approaches to the field. The editorial board comprises Geoffrey Khan, Aaron Hornkohl, and Esther-Miriam Wagner.

This is the first Open Access book series in the field; it combines the high peer-review and editorial standards with the fair Open Access model offered by OBP. Open Access (that is, making texts free to read and reuse) helps spread research results and other educational materials to everyone everywhere, not just to those who can afford it or have access to well-endowed university libraries.

Copyrights stay where they belong, with the authors. Authors are encouraged to secure funding to offset the publication costs and thereby sustain the publishing model, but if no institutional funding is available, authors are not charged for publication. Any grant secured covers the actual costs of publishing and is not taken as profit. In short: we support publishing that respects the authors and serves the public interest.

This book was copyedited by Anne Burberry.

Other titles of the series

An Introduction to Andalusi Hebrew Metrics

José Martínez Delgado

doi.org/10.11647/OBP.0351

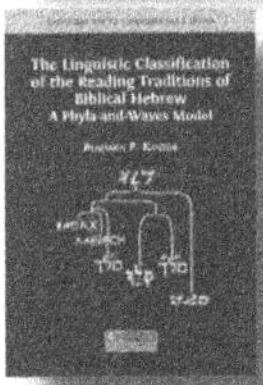

The Linguistic Classification of the Reading Traditions of Biblical Hebrew: A Phyla-and-Waves Model

Benjamin Paul Kantor

doi.org/10.11647/OBP.0210

UNIVERSITY OF CAMBRIDGE
Faculty of Asian and Middle Eastern Studies

More information and a complete list of books in this series can be found at:
https://www.openbookpublishers.com/series/2632-6914

www.ingramcontent.com/pod-product-compliance
Lightning Source LLC
Chambersburg PA
CBHW050524170426
43201CB00013B/2070
* 9 7 8 1 8 0 5 1 1 1 8 2 5 *